Better Homes and Gardens®
fish & seafood
COOKING FOR TODAY

BETTER HOMES AND GARDENS® BOOKS
Des Moines

BETTER HOMES AND GARDENS® BOOKS
An Imprint of Meredith® Books
President, Book Group: Joseph J. Ward
Vice President and Editorial Director: Elizabeth P. Rice
Executive Editor: Nancy N. Green
Managing Editor: Christopher Cavanaugh
Art Director: Ernest Shelton
Test Kitchen Director: Sharon Stilwell

FISH & SEAFOOD
Editor: Mary Major Williams
Writer: Martha Schiel
Recipe Development: Maryellyn Krantz, Diane Ward
Associate Art Director: Tom Wegner
Graphic Production Coordinator: Paula Forest
Production Manager: Doug Johnston
Test Kitchen Product Supervisor: Marilyn Cornelius
Food Stylists: Lynn Blanchard, Janet Pittman, Jennifer Peterson
Photographers: Mike Dieter, Scott Little
Cover Photographer: Andy Lyons

On the cover: Sweet Pepper Salsa Fish (see recipe, page 48)

Meredith Corporation Corporate Officers:
Chairman of the Executive Committee: E. T. Meredith III
Chairman of the Board, President and Chief Executive Officer: Jack D. Rehm
Group Presidents: Joseph J. Ward, Books; William T. Kerr, Magazines; Philip A. Jones, Broadcasting;
    Allen L. Sabbag, Real Estate
Vice Presidents: Leo R. Armatis, Corporate Relations; Thomas G. Fisher, General Counsel and Secretary;
    Larry D. Hartsook, Finance; Michael A. Sell, Treasurer; Kathleen J. Zehr, Controller and Assistant Secretary

WE CARE!

All of us at Better Homes and Gardens® Books are dedicated to providing you with the information
and ideas you need to create tasty foods. We welcome your comments and suggestions. Write us at:
Better Homes and Gardens® Books, Cookbook Editorial Department, LN-126, 1716 Locust St.,
Des Moines, IA 50309-3023

Our seal assures you that every recipe in *Fish & Seafood*
has been tested in the Better Homes and Gardens® Test
Kitchen. This means that each recipe is practical and
reliable, and meets our high standards of taste appeal.
We guarantee your satisfaction with this book for as long
as you own it.

It's fresh, it's fabulous—it's fish!

More and more health conscious people are choosing fish and seafood for their meals because of the low-fat content. But fish also suits our hectic lifestyles. Fish is quick to cook, relatively inexpensive, readily available, and can be prepared to please the pickiest of palates.

Some of the prize catches you'll find in this book include swordfish topped with a tropical spicy mango and avocado salsa, orange roughy in a gingered sesame sauce, bulgur-stuffed salmon steaks grilled over apple wood chips, and simple poached snapper in a fresh lemon and dill sauce.

We haven't neglected shellfish either. Try a creamy Havarti-filled lobster tail with a hint of fragrant basil, shrimp smothered in a creamy peanut and chili sauce, or a smooth crab mornay served in crisp pastry shells.

No longer does it matter whether you live on the coast or find yourself land-locked in the midwest. Celebrate the rich diversity and versatility of fish today and start reeling in the compliments.

CONTENTS

STORING FISH

When it comes to fresh fish, the sooner cooked, the better. When you bring fresh fish home from the market, wrap it loosely in clear plastic wrap and refrigerate. Use the fish within 2 days. If you don't plan to use the fish right away, wrap uncooked fish in moisture- and vapor-proof wrap and freeze for up to 3 months.

To thaw fish, place unwrapped fish in the refrigerator for 6 to 8 hours. Or, place 1 pound frozen fillets or steaks in a microwave-safe baking dish. Cover with vented plastic wrap. Micro-cook on 30% power (medium-low) for 6 to 8 minutes, turning and separating fish after 3 minutes. Let fillets stand 10 minutes and steaks stand 15 minutes. Fish should be pliable and cold on the outside, slightly icy in the center of thick areas. Rinse the fish and pat dry. Do not thaw fish at room temperature or in water because it will not thaw evenly and may spoil. Never refreeze fish.

TESTING FOR DONENESS

There's no subsitute for perfectly cooked fish. And although fish is easy to cook, it calls for careful attention during cooking because it cooks very quickly. To test fish for doneness, stick the tines of a fork into the thickest portion of the fish at a 45° angle. Then gently twist the fork and pull up some of the flesh. Properly cooked fish is opaque and has milky white juices. The flesh flakes easily with a fork and separates from any bones present. Undercooked fish is translucent and has clear, watery juices. The flesh is firm and does not flake easily. If the fish is not done, continue cooking till it flakes easily with a fork. Overcooked fish is opaque and has little, if any juices. The fish breaks into small pieces and looks dry.

BUYING SEAFOOD

Buying seafood may seem tricky at first, but becomes simple once you know what to look for. Here are some pointers.
Shrimp: Available raw or cooked, fresh or frozen, shelled or in the shell, or canned. Shrimp are sold by size or count per pound. The larger the shrimp, the more expensive they are. Fresh shrimp have a mild aroma and firm meat. The shell color may be shades of white, gray, brown, or pink.
Scallops: Available fresh or frozen, scallops have a sweet smell. The major types of scallops are the small bay scallop and the large bay scallop. A scallop's color varies with the food it ate and minerals in its water.
Crabs: Available live, cooked in the shell, cooked and frozen whole or as legs and claws, canned, or canned pasteurized; the latter of which requires refrigeration. Fresh cooked crab or canned crab is available as lump or flake meat. The lump meat consists of choice nuggets of white meat. Flake meat is smaller pieces.
Clams and Oysters: Available live, shucked or canned. Look for fresh ones that are plump and have clear juices.The shells should close tightly when tapped.
Frozen Seafood-Flavored Fish or "Surimi:" Readily available and less expensive than seafood, this product is made of fish that has been processed to look and taste like crab or lobster.

SELECTING FISH

There are so many varieties of fish available it helps to know their characteristics. That way you can experiment with different types of fish in the recipes, making the most of the ones available in your supermarket or fish market.

Fish	Flavor	Texture	Fat Content	Substitutions
Cod	Delicate	Firm	Low	Haddock, Halibut, Pike, Pollock
Croaker	Mild	Firm	Low	Cod, Cusk, Drum
Cusk	Delicate	Firm	Low	Catfish, Cod, Croaker
Flounder	Delicate to mild	Fine	Low	Pike, Sole, Whitefish, Whiting
Grouper	Mild	Firm	Low	Cod, Monkfish, Sea Bass
Haddock	Delicate	Firm	Low	Cod, Halibut, Lake Trout, Sole, Whitefish
Monkfish	Mild	Firm	Low	Cusk
Mullet	Mild to moderate	Firm	Moderate to high	Substitution not recommended
Orange Roughy	Delicate	Firm	Low	Cod, Flounder, Sea Bass, Sole
Pike (Walleye)	Mild to Moderate	Firm	Low	Cod, Orange Roughy, Whitefish
Pollock	Mild to Moderate	Firm	Low to Moderate	Cod, Flounder, Pike
Red Snapper	Mild to Moderate	Firm	Low	Lake Trout, Rockfish, Whitefish
Rockfish	Mild to Moderate	Firm, Chewy	Low	Cod, Drum, Ocean Perch, Red Snapper
Salmon	Mild to Moderate	Firm	Moderate to High	Swordfish, Tuna
Sea Bass	Delicate to Mild	Firm	Moderate	Cod, Orange Roughy, Sea Trout
Sole	Delicate to Mild	Fine	Low	Flounder, Pike
Swordfish	Mild to Moderate	Firm, Dense	Low to Moderate	Sea Bass, Shark, Tuna
Trout (Lake)	Mild	Firm	Moderate to High	Pike, Sea Trout, Whitefish
Trout (Rainbow)	Delicate	Firm	Moderate to High	Coho Salmon, Pike, Sea Trout
Tuna	Mild to Moderate	Firm	Moderate to High	Mackerel, Salmon, Swordfish
Whiting	Delicate	Firm	Low	Flounder, Pike, Pollock, Sole

PESTO SOLE ROLL-UPS

Walleye pike is often called the "sole" of fresh waters and has long been a favorite of fishermen. It works equally as well as sole or flounder in these carrot and pesto filled bundles.

4   **4-ounce fresh *or* frozen sole *or* flounder fillets (¼ to ½ inch thick)**
⅔   **cup refrigerated pesto sauce**
1   **medium carrot, finely shredded (½ cup)**
1   **tablespoon margarine *or* butter, melted**
3   **tablespoons fine dry bread crumbs**
1   **teaspoon finely shredded lemon peel**
6   **ounces hot cooked fettuccine**
1   **tablespoon lemon juice**
    Lemon wedges (optional)
    Carrot curls (optional)
    Basil leaves (optional)

Thaw fish, if frozen. Rinse fish; pat dry with paper towels.

Spread *one* side of *each* fish fillet with about *1 tablespoon* of the pesto. Sprinkle *each* with *2 tablespoons* of the shredded carrot. Roll up fillets from short sides; secure with wooden toothpicks. Place fish rolls in a 2-quart square baking dish. Brush with melted margarine or butter.

Toss together fine dry bread crumbs and lemon peel; sprinkle over fish rolls. Bake, uncovered, in a 375° oven for 20 to 25 minutes or till fish flakes easily with a fork.

Toss together remaining pesto, hot fettuccini, and lemon juice. Divide pasta mixture evenly among four plates and top each with one fish roll. If desired, garnish with lemon wedges, carrot curls, and basil leaves. Makes 4 servings.

Nutrition information per serving: 607 calories, 31 g protein, 47 g carbohydrate, 32 g fat (1 g saturated), 59 mg cholesterol, 475 mg sodium, 365 mg potassium.

ISLAND SWORDFISH

A spicy mango-and-avocado salsa, fragrant with a dash of lime and chili, adds a truly tropical taste.

4	4-ounce fresh *or* frozen swordfish steaks (about ¾ inch thick)
½	cup chopped fresh *or* canned mango *or* frozen peaches, thawed
¼	cup chopped avocado
¼	medium red sweet pepper, chopped (¼ cup)
½	small red onion, chopped (2 tablespoons)
1	teaspoon finely shredded lime *or* lemon peel (set aside)
6	tablespoons lime *or* lemon juice
1	tablespoon snipped fresh cilantro *or* parsley
1	teaspoon grated gingerroot *or* ¼ teaspoon ground ginger
2	cloves garlic, minced
	Dash bottled hot pepper sauce (optional)
3	tablespoons dry white wine
1	tablespoon orange liqueur (optional)
½	teaspoon pepper
	Green onions (optional)

Thaw fish, if frozen. Rinse fish; pat dry with paper towels. Set aside.

For fruit salsa, in a bowl stir together mango or peaches, avocado, red pepper, onion, *2 tablespoons* lime or lemon juice, cilantro or parsley, ginger, garlic, and, if desired, hot pepper sauce. Cover and chill. (Let salsa stand at room temperature 20 minutes before serving.)

For marinade, in a small bowl stir together the remaining lime or lemon juice, lime or lemon peel, wine, orange liqueur (if desired), and pepper. Place fish steaks in a shallow dish. Pour marinade over fish. Cover and chill for 1 hour, turning fish occasionally.

Drain fish; discard marinade. Place fish steaks on the greased unheated rack of a broiling pan. Broil 4 to 5 inches from the heat for 8 to 12 minutes or till fish flakes easily with a fork, turning once during cooking. To serve, top fish steaks with fruit salsa. If desired, garnish with green onions. Makes 4 servings.

Nutrition information per serving: 186 calories, 23 g protein, 7 g carbohydrate, 7 g fat (2 g saturated), 45 mg cholesterol, 105 mg sodium, 487 mg potassium.

GROUPER WITH SUMMER VEGETABLES

If you choose the green pepper option, use a red onion to brighten the vegetable mixture.

1 pound fresh *or* frozen grouper fillets
(½ to ¾ inch thick)
2 tablespoons lemon juice
1 tablespoon margarine *or* butter,
melted
½ teaspoon dried marjoram *or* basil,
crushed
⅛ to ¼ teaspoon ground red pepper
1 medium onion, chopped (½ cup)
½ medium red *or* green sweet pepper,
chopped (½ cup)
½ small zucchini, chopped (½ cup)
½ small yellow summer squash, chopped
(½ cup)
1 tablespoon cooking oil
2 tablespoons snipped parsley
¼ teaspoon garlic salt
¼ teaspoon dried marjoram *or* basil,
crushed
Fresh marjoram sprigs (optional)

Thaw fish, if frozen. Cut into 4 serving-size portions. Rinse fish; pat dry with paper towels. Place fish fillets in a 2-quart rectangular baking dish. Set aside.

In a small bowl stir together lemon juice, melted margarine or butter, the ½ teaspoon marjoram or basil, and the ground red pepper. Drizzle fish with lemon juice mixture. Bake, uncovered, in a 450° oven till fish flakes easily with a fork (allow 4 to 6 minutes per ½-inch thickness of fish).

Meanwhile, in a medium skillet cook onion, red or green sweet pepper, zucchini, and yellow summer squash in hot oil for 2 to 3 minutes or till just crisp-tender. Stir in parsley, garlic salt and the ¼ teaspoon marjoram or basil. Serve vegetables over fish. Garnish with fresh marjoram, if desired. Makes 4 servings.

Nutrition information per serving: 179 calories, 23 g protein, 5 g carbohydrate, 8 g fat (1 g saturated), 42 mg cholesterol, 211 mg sodium, 546 mg potassium.

FRUITED COUSCOUS-STUFFED SALMON ROAST

For a colorful stuffing choose a red pear and leave the peel on it. From another pear, cut some thin wedges to garnish this stunning salmon.

1   stalk celery, chopped (½ cup)
1   medium onion, chopped (½ cup)
1   tablespoon margarine *or* butter
⅔   cup chicken broth
½   cup apple cider *or* apple juice
½   teaspoon ground coriander
¼   teaspoon ground allspice
⅛   teaspoon pepper
1½ cups corn bread stuffing mix
1½ cups chopped pear
½   cup couscous
½   cup light raisins
¼   cup snipped parsley
1   3-pound fresh salmon roast (about 8 inches long and 2¼ inches thick), boned, *or* one 4- to 5-pound whole dressed salmon (with head and tail)
1   tablespoon cooking oil
    Pear wedges (optional)
    Celery leaves (optional)

For stuffing, in a medium saucepan cook celery and onion in margarine or butter till onion is tender but not brown; remove from heat. Stir in chicken broth, apple cider or apple juice, coriander, allspice, and pepper.

In a medium bowl combine stuffing mix, chopped pear, couscous, raisins, and parsley. Add celery mixture; toss lightly to mix.

Rinse fish; pat dry with paper towels. Fill fish cavity with *1 cup* of the stuffing. Tie or skewer fish closed. Place stuffed fish on a greased rack in a large shallow baking pan. Place the remaining stuffing in a 1-quart casserole; cover casserole.

Brush outside of fish with oil; cover loosely with foil. Bake fish and stuffing in a 350° oven about 50 minutes for a salmon roast (50 to 60 minutes for a whole dressed salmon) or till fish flakes easily with a fork and stuffing is heated through. Garnish with pear wedges and celery leaves, if desired. Makes 8 servings.

Nutrition information per serving: 361 calories, 29 g protein, 39 g carbohydrate, 10 g fat (2 g saturated), 31 mg cholesterol, 375 mg sodium, 465 mg potassium.

HALIBUT WITH CREAMY DIJON SAUCE

Feel like having a barbecue instead of cooking these fish steaks indoors? Grill the fish on an oiled rack directly over medium-hot coals for 5 minutes. Turn fish, brush with the brushing sauce, and grill for 3 to 7 minutes more or till fish is done.

1½	pounds fresh *or* frozen halibut *or* sea bass steaks, about 1 inch thick
1	tablespoon margarine *or* butter, melted
¼	teaspoon onion salt
¼	teaspoon dried marjoram, crushed
¼	teaspoon dried thyme, crushed
½	cup dairy sour cream
1	tablespoon all-purpose flour
1	tablespoon Dijon-style mustard
⅛	teaspoon salt
⅛	teaspoon pepper
⅛	teaspoon dried thyme, crushed
½	cup chicken *or* vegetable broth
4	cups shredded fresh spinach (5 ounces)
1	medium carrot, shredded (½ cup)
	Lemon wedges (optional)

Thaw fish, if frozen. Rinse fish; pat dry with paper towels. Cut into serving size pieces, if necessary. Set aside.

For brushing sauce, combine melted margarine or butter, onion salt, marjoram, and the ¼ teaspoon thyme.

Place fish steaks on the rack of an unheated broiler pan. Brush fish steaks with brushing sauce. Broil 4 inches from the heat for 5 minutes. Turn fish. Brush with remaining brushing sauce. Broil for 3 to 7 minutes more or till fish flakes easily with a fork.

Meanwhile, for Dijon sauce, in a small saucepan stir together the sour cream, flour, mustard, salt, pepper, and the ⅛ teaspoon thyme. Add chicken or vegetable broth, stirring till well mixed. Cook and stir over medium heat till mixture is thickened and bubbly. Cook and stir for 1 minute more. Keep warm.

Toss together spinach and carrot. Line individual plates with the spinach mixture. Serve fish on spinach mixture. Top with Dijon sauce. Garnish with lemon wedges, if desired. Makes 4 servings.

Nutrition information per serving: 282 calories, 39 g protein, 9 g carbohydrate, 9 g fat (2 g saturated), 59 mg cholesterol, 549 mg sodium, 1,048 mg potassium.

TROUT AMANDINE

Cooked bias-sliced carrots and sprigs of bright green parsley complement the classic garnish of sautéed almonds.

4   **8 to 10-ounce pan-dressed trout**
⅓   **cup all-purpose flour**
¼   **teaspoon salt**
¼   **teaspoon pepper**
¼   **cup milk *or* buttermilk**
3   **tablespoons cooking oil**
2   **tablespoons margarine *or* butter**
¼   **cup sliced almonds**
1   **tablespoon lemon juice**
1   **tablespoon snipped parsley**

Rinse trout; pat dry with paper towels. Set aside.

In a shallow dish combine flour, salt, and pepper. Place milk or buttermilk in a shallow dish. Dip trout into milk and then into flour mixture, turning to coat both sides.

In a 12-inch skillet heat oil and *1 tablespoon* of the margarine or butter over medium heat; add *two* of the trout. Fry for 5 to 7 minutes or till golden. Turn carefully and fry for 5 to 7 minutes more or till meat flakes easily with a fork. Drain trout on paper towels. Keep warm in a 300° oven. Fry remaining trout, adding additional oil and margarine or butter as necessary.

Drain and scrape drippings from skillet; discard. Add 1 tablespoon margarine or butter and almonds to skillet; cook and stir over medium heat for 2 minutes or till almonds are golden. Remove from heat. Carefully stir in lemon juice and parsley. Spoon almond mixture over fish. Makes 4 servings.

Nutrition information per serving: 493 calories, 50 g protein, 10 g carbohydrate, 27 g fat (5 g saturated), 131 mg cholesterol, 136 mg sodium, 1,225 mg potassium.

DEEP-DISH TUNA PIE

A convenient, off-the-shelf piecrust mix makes a flaky top that looks and tastes like you made it from scratch.

½   of an 11-ounce package piecrust mix
     (1⅓ cups)
1   large onion, chopped (1 cup)
1   medium potato, peeled and diced
     (about 1 cup)
¼   cup water
1   10¾-ounce can condensed cream of
     mushroom soup
⅓   cup milk
⅓   cup grated Parmesan cheese
1   tablespoon lemon juice
¾   teaspoon dried dillweed
¼   teaspoon pepper
1   16-ounce package frozen mixed
     vegetables
1   9¼-ounce can tuna, drained and
     broken into chunks
1   beaten egg

Prepare piecrust mix according to package directions *except* do not roll out. Cover dough; set aside.

In a large skillet cook onion and potato in a small amount of water, covered, about 7 minutes or till tender. Drain off liquid. Stir in soup, milk, Parmesan cheese, lemon juice, dillweed, and pepper. Cook and stir till mixture is bubbly. Gently stir in frozen mixed vegetables and tuna. Spoon mixture into an ungreased 2-quart casserole.

On a lightly floured surface roll pastry into a circle 2 inches larger than the diameter of the top of the casserole and about ⅛ inch thick. Make 1-inch slits near the center of the pastry. Center pastry over top of casserole, allowing ends to hang over edge. Trim pastry ½ inch beyond edge of casserole. Turn pastry under; flute to the casserole edge, pressing gently. Brush pastry with beaten egg.

Bake in a 400° oven for 40 to 45 minutes or till crust is golden brown. Serve immediately. Makes 6 servings.

Nutrition information per serving: 386 calories, 21 g protein, 35 g carbohydrate, 18 g fat (5 g saturated), 49 mg cholesterol, 893 mg sodium, 470 mg potassium.

FISH CREOLE

Halibut, haddock, or orange roughy are excellent choices for this saucy rice combo.

1 pound fresh *or* frozen skinless, firm-fleshed fish fillets
1 medium onion, chopped (½ cup)
1 stalk celery, chopped (½ cup)
½ medium green pepper, chopped (½ cup)
2   cloves garlic, minced *or* ¼ teaspoon garlic powder
2 tablespoons margarine *or* butter
1 16-ounce can tomatoes, cut up
¼ cup water
2 tablespoons tomato paste
1 tablespoon snipped parsley
1 teaspoon instant chicken bouillon granules
1 teaspoon chili powder
½ teaspoon Worcestershire sauce
   Several dashes bottled hot pepper sauce
1 10-ounce package frozen cut okra
2 cups hot cooked rice
   Lemon wedges (optional)

Thaw fish, if frozen. Rinse fish; pat dry with paper towels. Cut fish into 1-inch pieces; set aside.

In a large skillet cook onion, celery, green pepper, and garlic in margarine or butter till tender but not brown.

Add *undrained* tomatoes, water, tomato paste, parsley, bouillon granules, chili powder, Worcestershire sauce, and hot pepper sauce. Bring mixture to boiling; reduce heat. Simmer, uncovered, for 5 minutes.

Add fish and okra to tomato mixture, stirring gently to mix. Return mixture to boiling; reduce heat. Cover and simmer for 5 minutes or till fish flakes easily with a fork. Serve over hot cooked rice. Garnish with lemon wedges, if desired. Makes 4 servings.

Nutrition information per serving: 379 calories, 30 g protein, 44 g carbohydrate, 9 g fat (2 g saturated), 36 mg cholesterol, 626 mg sodium, 1,222 mg potassium.

FLOUNDER WITH GINGER-DILL SAUCE

Because of its delicate flavor, dill is often matched with fish. And its feathery leaves make an attractive garnish.

1 pound fresh *or* frozen flounder, sole, *or* cod fillets
⅓ cup mayonnaise *or* salad dressing
2 tablespoons dairy sour cream
1 teaspoon grated gingerroot *or* ¼ teaspoon ground ginger
1 teaspoon snipped fresh dill *or* ¼ teaspoon dried dillweed
½ teaspoon dried minced onion
¼ cup frozen peeled, cooked small shrimp, thawed, *or* drained canned small shrimp
1 tablespoon margarine *or* butter
8 frozen peeled, cooked small shrimp, thawed, *or* drained canned small shrimp (optional)
  Lemon slices (optional)
  Fresh dill (optional)

Thaw fish, if frozen. Measure thickness of fish fillets. Rinse fish; pat dry with paper towels. Set aside.

For sauce, in a small bowl stir together the mayonnaise or salad dressing, sour cream, ginger, dill, and onion. Stir in ¼ cup shrimp; set sauce aside.

Place fish fillets in a 2-quart rectangular baking dish. Dot with margarine or butter. Bake in a 450° oven till fish flakes easily with a fork (allow 6 to 8 minutes per ½-inch thickness of fish). Spoon sauce over fish. Garnish with additional shrimp, lemon slices, and fresh dill, if desired. Makes 4 servings.

Nutrition information per serving: 268 calories, 21 g protein, 1 g carbohydrate, 20 g fat (4 g saturated), 76 mg cholesterol, 225 mg sodium, 240 mg potassium.

SESAME ORANGE ROUGHY

To make onion brushes, slice roots from ends of green onions and remove most of the green portion. Slash the remaining green portion to make a fringe. Then, place in ice water for a few minutes to curl the ends.

1   **pound fresh *or* frozen orange roughy
       or other fish fillets (¾ inch thick)**
2   **tablespoons lime juice**
1   **tablespoon margarine *or* butter**
2   **tablespoons water**
4   **teaspoons soy sauce**
2   **teaspoons honey**
1   **clove garlic, minced**
½   **teaspoon grated gingerroot *or*
       ⅛ teaspoon ground ginger**
½   **teaspoon toasted sesame oil**
½   **teaspoon lime *or* lemon juice**
¼   **teaspoon pepper**
1   **green onion, sliced
       (about 1 tablespoon)**
2   **teaspoons sesame seed, toasted**

Thaw fish, if frozen. Cut fillets into 4 serving-size portions. Rinse fish; pat dry with paper towels; set aside.

Brush both sides of fillets with the 2 tablespoons lime juice. In a large skillet heat margarine or butter over medium heat till melted. Add fillets; cook for 5 minutes. Turn carefully and cook for 3 to 5 minutes more or till fish flakes easily with a fork. Remove skillet from heat. Transfer fish to serving plates; keep warm.

Meanwhile, in a small bowl stir together water, soy sauce, honey, garlic, ginger, toasted sesame oil, the ½ teaspoon lime or lemon juice, and pepper.

Carefully pour soy sauce mixture into skillet; return skillet to heat. Heat soy mixture through, scraping up browned bits from bottom of skillet. Pour soy mixture over fish. Sprinkle with chopped green onion and sesame seed. Makes 4 servings.

Nutrition information per serving: 269 calories, 21 g protein, 33 g carbohydrate, 5 g fat (1 g saturated), 23 mg cholesterol, 453 mg sodium, 78 mg potassium.

FISH À LA DIABLE

If the fish fillets are small, overlap two or three to make one four-ounce serving. If they're too large, cut them into into serving size portions.

4 fresh *or* frozen croaker, mullet, flounder, whiting, turbot, *or* pollack fillets (1 pound)
2 medium carrots
1 cup sliced fresh mushrooms
⅓ cup sliced celery
½ cup plain yogurt
1 to 2 tablespoons Dijon-style mustard
½ medium red sweet pepper, thinly sliced into strips (½ cup)
½ medium green pepper, thinly sliced into strips (½ cup)
1 tablespoon margarine *or* butter, melted
1 teaspoon all-purpose flour
3 tablespoons milk
   Fresh dill (optional)
   Lemon wedges, halved (optional)

Thaw fish, if frozen. Rinse fish; pat dry with paper towels. Set aside.

Cut each carrot into 4 long strips (8 strips total). In a medium saucepan cook carrots, mushrooms, and celery in a small amount of boiling water for 5 minutes or just till tender. Drain; separating carrots from mushrooms and celery. Set vegetables aside.

Combine the yogurt and mustard; set aside ⅓ *cup* of the mustard mixture. Brush the remaining mustard mixture over one side of each fillet. Lay *one-fourth* of the red and green pepper strips and *two* carrot strips crosswise on mustard side of *each* fillet. Starting from a short end, roll up fish around vegetables.

Arrange fish rolls, seam side down, in a 9x9x2-inch baking pan. Brush with melted margarine or butter. Bake, uncovered, in a 400° oven for 15 to 20 minutes or till fish flakes easily with a fork.

Meanwhile, for sauce, in a small saucepan stir flour into reserved ⅓ cup mustard mixture; stir in milk. Add cooked mushrooms and celery. Cook and stir over medium heat till mixture is thickened and bubbly; cook and stir for 1 minute more. Remove from heat.

Transfer fish rolls to dinner plates. Spoon sauce over fish. Garnish with fresh dill and halved lemon wedges, if desired. Makes 4 servings.

Nutrition information per serving: 361 calories, 26 g protein, 19 g carbohydrate, 20 g fat (5 g saturated), 107 mg cholesterol, 630 mg sodium, 747 mg potassium.

BAKED HADDOCK WITH MUSHROOM SAUCE

A sprinkle of lemon-pepper seasoning enhances the delicate flavor of haddock in this simple dish.

1 pound fresh *or* frozen haddock *or* cod
    fillets
   Lemon-pepper seasoning
2 cups sliced fresh mushrooms
2 to 3 green onions, sliced (⅓ cup)
1 tablespoon margarine *or* butter
⅓ cup chicken broth
¼ cup dry white wine *or* chicken broth
2 teaspoons cornstarch

Thaw fish, if frozen. Measure thickness of fillets. Cut fish fillets into 4 serving-size portions. Rinse fish; pat dry with paper towels.

Place fish fillets in a 2-quart rectangular baking dish; sprinkle with lemon-pepper seasoning. Bake, uncovered, in a 450° oven till fish flakes easily with a fork (allow 4 to 6 minutes per ½-inch thickness).

Meanwhile, for mushroom sauce, in a small saucepan cook mushrooms and green onions in margarine or butter till tender. Stir together chicken broth, wine or chicken broth, and cornstarch; add to mushroom mixture all at once. Cook and stir till mixture is thickened and bubbly; cook and stir for 2 minutes more.

Transfer fish fillets to serving plates; spoon mushroom sauce over fish. Makes 4 servings.

Nutrition information per serving: 200 calories, 19 g protein, 9 g carbohydrate, 8 g fat (2 g saturated), 44 mg cholesterol, 323 mg sodium, 475 mg potassium.

ALMOND-STUFFED FLOUNDER WITH CREAMY TARRAGON SAUCE

If you prefer, cook three ounces of fettuccine or linguine to serve under these fancy fish rolls in place of the wild rice. Choose a tomato or spinach pasta for added color and flavor.

2 4-ounce fresh *or* frozen flounder *or* sole fillets (¼ to ½ inch thick)
½ cup shredded Swiss cheese (2 ounces)
2 tablespoons chopped almonds
1 tablespoon snipped chives
2 tablespoons margarine *or* butter, softened
Paprika
¼ cup dry white wine
¼ cup shredded carrot
2 teaspoons all-purpose flour
⅛ teaspoon dried tarragon, crushed
Dash salt
Dash white pepper
½ cup milk
1 cup hot cooked wild rice
Fresh tarragon (optional)

Thaw fish, if frozen. Rinse fish; pat dry with paper towels. Set aside.

For stuffing, in a small bowl combine *half* of the Swiss cheese, the almonds, chives, and *1 tablespoon* of the margarine or butter.

Spoon *half* of the stuffing onto one end of *each* piece of fish. Roll up fish around the stuffing. Place fish, seam side down, in a small baking dish. Sprinkle with paprika. Pour *3 tablespoons* of the wine into the dish. Bake, uncovered, in a 375° oven for 15 minutes or till fish flakes easily with a fork.

Meanwhile, for sauce, in a small saucepan cook carrot in the remaining margarine or butter for 3 to 4 minutes or till tender. Stir in the flour, tarragon, salt, and white pepper; add milk all at once. Cook and stir till mixture is thickened and bubbly. Stir in remaining Swiss cheese and remaining wine.

To serve, place fish rolls atop hot cooked wild rice; top with sauce. Garnish with fresh tarragon, if desired. Makes 2 servings.

Nutrition information per serving: 542 calories, 34 g protein, 27 g carbohydrate, 31 g fat (10 g saturated), 84 mg cholesterol, 465 mg sodium, 617 mg potassium.

NUTTY PARMESAN FISH

A light and crispy coating that features cracker crumbs, pine nuts, and Parmesan cheese makes a flavor-packed breading for these oven-fried fish sticks.

1   pound fresh *or* frozen orange roughy
    fillets
1   beaten egg
2   tablespoons milk
¼   cup finely crushed rich round crackers
2   tablespoons grated Parmesan cheese
2   tablespoons ground pine nuts *or*
    almonds
½   teaspoon dried basil, crushed
⅛   teaspoon pepper
2   tablespoons margarine *or* butter,
    melted
    Tartar Sauce (optional)

Thaw fish, if frozen. Measure thickness of fillets. Cut fish fillets into 1-inch wide strips. Rinse and pat dry with paper towels; set aside.

In a shallow dish combine egg and milk. In another shallow dish combine cracker crumbs, Parmesan cheese, ground nuts, basil, and pepper. Dip fish pieces into egg mixture. Then roll fish in crumb mixture. Place coated fish in a greased shallow baking pan.

Drizzle melted margarine or butter over fish. Bake in a 500° oven till coating is golden and fish flakes easily with a fork (allow 4 to 6 minutes per ½-inch of thickness of fish). If desired, serve with Tartar Sauce. Makes 4 servings.

Tartar Sauce: In a small mixing bowl stir together 1 cup *mayonnaise or salad dressing*, ¼ cup finely *chopped dill pickle or sweet pickle relish*, 1 tablespoon sliced *green onion*, 1 tablespoon snipped *parsley*, 1 tablespoon diced *pimiento*, and 1 teaspoon *lemon juice.* Cover and chill till serving. Makes 1 cup.

Nutrition information per serving: 221 calories, 22 g protein, 5 g carbohydrate, 13 g fat (3 g saturated), 80 mg cholesterol, 267 mg sodium, 71 mg potassium.

BULGUR-STUFFED SALMON STEAKS

Grilling over apple wood chips imparts a light, fruity smoked flavor to the salmon steaks making the extra effort well worthwhile.

4   fresh *or* frozen salmon steaks,
    cut 1 inch thick (about 2 pounds)
2   cups apple wood chips
1   cup boiling water
½   cup bulgur wheat
2   tablespoons snipped parsley
1   green onion, sliced (about
    1 tablespoon)
1½ teaspoons snipped fresh cilantro *or*
    ½ teaspoon ground coriander
¼   teaspoon salt
    Cooking oil
2   tablespoons lemon juice
2   tablespoons margarine *or* butter,
    melted

Thaw fish, if frozen; set aside.

About 1 hour before cooking, soak apple wood chips in enough water to cover; let stand.

In a small bowl combine boiling water and bulgur. Let stand for 30 minutes; drain. Stir together drained bulgur, parsley, green onion, cilantro, and salt. Set aside.

Form a 12x8x2-inch pan with heavy foil. Brush foil pan lightly with oil. Rinse fish; pat dry with paper towels. Place fish in a single layer in pan. Spoon *one-fourth* of the stuffing mixture into the center cavity of *each* steak. Combine lemon juice and melted margarine or butter; drizzle over salmon and stuffing.

In a covered grill, arrange medium-hot coals around edge of grill. Drain the apple wood chips; sprinkle over coals. Center foil pan on grill rack, not directly over coals; lower grill hood. Grill for 25 to 30 minutes or till the fish flakes easily with a fork. Makes 4 servings.

Nutrition information per serving: 331 calories, 35 g protein, 14 g carbohydrate, 15 g fat (3 g saturated), 41 mg cholesterol, 344 mg sodium, 408 mg potassium.

ITALIAN FISH PORTIONS

Keep this saucy dish in mind for days when you're short on time.

6 2- to 3-ounce frozen crumb-coated *or* battered-fried fish fillets
1 cup sliced fresh mushrooms
1 tablespoon cooking oil
1 tablespoon cornstarch
1 14½-ounce can Italian-style stewed tomatoes, cut up
⅛ teaspoon pepper
3 tablespoons grated Parmesan cheese
2 cups hot cooked pasta *or* rice

Bake fish fillets according to package directions.

Meanwhile, in a medium saucepan cook mushrooms in hot oil till tender. Stir in cornstarch; add *undrained* tomatoes and pepper. Cook and stir till mixture is thickened and bubbly. Cook and stir for 2 minutes more. Remove from heat.

To serve, spoon hot tomato mixture over fish. Sprinkle with Parmesan cheese. Serve with pasta or rice. Makes 6 servings.

Nutrition information per serving: 312 calories, 15 g protein, 40 g carbohydrate, 11 g fat (3 g saturated), 66 mg cholesterol, 628 mg sodium, 446 mg potassium.

BAKED SOLE AND CORN SALSA

Cilantro, also known as coriander and Chinese parsley, looks like parsley but packs a far more pungent flavour. Use it sparingly if you're not used to it.

1   **pound fresh *or* frozen sole *or* flounder fillets (about ¼ inch thick)**
1½ **cups salsa**
½   **cup frozen whole kernel corn**
    Fresh cilantro *or* parsley sprigs (optional)

Thaw fish, if frozen. Cut fish into 4 serving-size portions. Rinse fish; pat dry with paper towels. Arrange fish in a greased 2-quart rectangular baking dish, turning under any thin edges. Set aside.

In a small bowl combine the salsa and frozen corn; spoon over fish. Bake, uncovered, in a 375° oven for 10 to 15 minutes or till fish flakes easily with a fork. Using a slotted spatula, transfer fish and salsa topping to dinner plates. Garnish with cilantro or parsley sprigs, if desired. Makes 4 servings.

Nutrition information per serving: 138 calories, 21 g protein, 10 g carbohydrate, 4 g fat (0 g saturated), 53 mg cholesterol, 416 mg sodium, 573 mg potassium.

POACHED FISH WITH LEMON-DILL SAUCE

Using the poaching liquid from the fish adds a richness to the citrus sauce and salvages some of the vitamins and minerals that have been lost in the cooking process.

1   2- to 2½-pound fresh *or* frozen dressed
    red snapper *or* whitefish (head and
    tail removed)
2   cups vegetable broth, chicken broth
    or water
3   lemon slices
1   to 2 green onions, sliced
    (about 2 tablespoons)
1   tablespoon snipped fresh parsley *or*
    1 teaspoon dried parsley flakes
1   bay leaf
1   teaspoon lemon-pepper seasoning
2   tablespoons margarine *or* butter
4   teaspoons all-purpose flour
1   tablespoon snipped fresh dill *or*
    1 teaspoon dried dillweed
2   teaspoons lemon juice
1   egg yolk, beaten
    Fresh Dill (optional)

Thaw fish, if frozen. Rinse fish.

To poach, place fish on a large piece of 100% cotton cheesecloth; overlap cheesecloth on top of fish. Place fish on the rack of a poaching pan; set aside.

In the poaching pan, combine broth or water, lemon slices, green onion, parsley, bay leaf, and lemon-pepper seasoning. Heat broth mixture till boiling; add fish on rack. Reduce heat; cover and simmer for 20 to 30 minutes or till fish flakes easily with a fork (fold back cheesecloth to test the fish).

Transfer fish to a warm serving platter; keep warm. Strain the poaching liquid. Measure *1 cup* of the poaching liquid and reserve for sauce. Discard remaining liquid.

For sauce, in a small saucepan melt margarine or butter; stir in flour. Add the reserved poaching liquid, dill, and lemon juice. Cook and stir over medium heat till mixture is thickened and bubbly. Cook and stir for 1 minute more.

Gradually stir *half* of the hot mixture into the egg yolk; return egg mixture to the saucepan. Cook and stir till mixture is bubbly. Reduce heat; cook and stir for 1 to 2 minutes more. Serve sauce with fish. Garnish with fresh dill, if desired. Makes 4 servings.

Nutrition information per serving: 324 calories, 48 g protein, 6 g carbohydrate, 11 g fat (2 g saturated), 137 mg cholesterol, 645 mg sodium, 998 mg potassium.

SALMON AND VEGETABLE PIES

These individual, spaghetti-crust pies, brimming with chunks of salmon or tuna and lots of crisp vegetables, are sure to be winners with kids of all ages.

4   ounces spaghetti
1   beaten egg
⅓   cup grated Parmesan cheese
3   tablespoons margarine *or* butter
1   cup broccoli flowerets
1   medium carrot, thinly sliced (½ cup)
1   small onion, cut into thin wedges
½   teaspoon dried oregano *or* savory,
    crushed
1   clove garlic, minced
    Dash salt
1   12½-ounce can skinless, boneless
    salmon, drained and flaked, *or*
    one 9¼-ounce can tuna (water
    pack), drained and broken into
    chunks
2   beaten eggs
½   cup half-and-half, light cream, *or* milk

For spaghetti crusts, cook pasta according to package directions; drain. Immediately toss together pasta, 1 beaten egg, Parmesan cheese, and *1 tablespoon* of the margarine or butter. Divide pasta mixture evenly among 4 greased individual au gratin dishes. Press pasta mixture to sides and bottoms of dishes to form crusts. Set aside.

In a large skillet cook broccoli, carrot, onion, oregano or savory, garlic, and salt in the remaining margarine or butter till vegetables are crisp-tender. Gently stir salmon or tuna into the vegetable mixture.

Divide salmon mixture evenly between the four spaghetti crusts. Combine the 2 beaten eggs and half-and-half, light cream, or milk. Pour evenly over the salmon mixture. Cover with foil. Bake in a 350° oven for 15 minutes. Remove foil; bake for 5 to 10 minutes more or till set. Let stand for 5 minutes before serving. Makes 4 servings.

Nutrition information per serving: 472 calories, 33 g protein, 30 g carbohydrate, 24 g fat (8 g saturated), 212 mg cholesterol, 803 mg sodium, 594 mg potassium.

SWORDFISH EN SALSA VERDE

Tomatillos (toh-mah-TEE-yohs), an essential ingredient in salsa verde or "green salsa," are a small, olive-green fruit covered with a thin, brown, papery husk. They are a relative of the Cape gooseberry, not green tomatoes as many people think.

1¼ pounds swordfish *or* tuna steaks, ¾ to 1 inch thick

5 *or* 6 fresh tomatillos (6 ounces), husks removed, and finely chopped, *or* one 13-ounce can tomatillos, drained, rinsed, and finely chopped

½ small onion, finely chopped (2 tablespoons)

2 serrano *or* jalapeño peppers, seeded and finely chopped

1 tablespoon snipped fresh cilantro *or* parsley

1 teaspoon finely shredded lime peel *or* grapefruit peel

½ teaspoon sugar

¼ teaspoon salt

¼ teaspoon ground cumin

¼ teaspoon ground black pepper

1 tablespoon lime juice *or* grapefruit juice

½ avocado, seeded, peeled, and chopped

Tomato slices (optional)

Lime wedges (optional)

Cilantro *or* parsley (optional)

Thaw fish, if frozen. Cut into four serving-size portions, if necessary. Rinse fish; pat dry with paper towels. Set aside.

For salsa verde, in a medium bowl stir together tomatillos, onion, serrano or jalapeño peppers, cilantro or parsley, lime or grapefruit peel, and sugar. Set aside*.

In a small mixing bowl, combine salt, cumin, and black pepper; set aside. Place fish in a 3-quart rectangular glass baking dish. Brush fish with lime or grapefruit juice; sprinkle with cumin mixture. Stir avocado into salsa verde. Spoon salsa verde over fish.

Bake, uncovered, in a 450° oven for 6 to 12 minutes or till fish flakes easily with a fork. Transfer fish and salsa verde to dinner plates. Garnish with tomato slices, lime wedges, and cilantro or parsley, if desired. Makes 4 servings.

Note: Salsa verde may be made up to two days ahead of time. Store in a tightly covered container in the refrigerator.

Nutrition information per serving: 242 calories, 30 g protein, 7 g carbohydrate, 11 g fat (2 g saturated), 56 mg cholesterol, 265 mg sodium, 830 mg potassium.

FISH FILLETS AU GRATIN

Mild-tasting red snapper, rockfish, and whitefish are low in fat and have a firm texture—perfect for this delicately-flavored dish.

1 **pound fresh *or* frozen skinless fish fillets (¾ inch thick)**
¼ **cup fine dry bread crumbs**
2 **teaspoons snipped fresh dill *or* ½ teaspoon dried dillweed**
¼ **teaspoon dried tarragon, crushed**
¼ **teaspoon lemon-pepper seasoning**
½ **cup shredded cheddar cheese (2 ounces)**

Thaw fish, if frozen. Cut fish fillets into 4 serving-size portions. Rinse fish; pat dry with paper towels. Place fish fillets in a shallow baking dish; set aside.

In a small bowl combine bread crumbs, dill, tarragon, and lemon-pepper seasoning. Stir well.

Spoon bread crumb mixture over fish. Bake, uncovered, in a 400° oven for 20 to 25 minutes or till fish flakes easily with a fork. Sprinkle with cheese; bake for 3 to 5 minutes more or till cheese melts. Makes 4 servings.

Nutrition information per serving: 195 calories, 28 g protein, 5 g carbohydrate, 7 g fat (3 g saturated), 57 mg cholesterol, 252 mg sodium, 489 mg potassium.

SWEET PEPPER SALSA FISH
A garnish of fresh oregano leaves complements the flavor of the sautéed vegetable and salsa topping.

1 pound fresh *or* frozen skinless fish
   fillets (¾ inch thick)
2 tablespoons cooking oil
1½ cups fresh mushrooms, quartered
1 cup coarsely chopped green *and/or*
   yellow sweet pepper
1 small onion, halved and sliced
1 cup salsa
   Fresh oregano (optional)

Thaw fish, if frozen. Cut fish fillets into 4 serving-size portions, if necessary. Rinse fish; pat dry with paper towels; set aside.

In a large skillet heat *1 tablespoon* of the cooking oil. Cook mushrooms, green or yellow sweet pepper, and onion in the hot oil for 5 minutes or just till tender. Remove vegetables with a slotted spoon; set aside.

Add the remaining cooking oil to skillet. Add fish fillets. Cook over medium heat for 8 to 10 minutes or till fish flakes easily with a fork, turning once.

Spoon the cooked vegetables over fish fillets. Top with salsa. Cover and cook over low heat about 2 minutes or till heated through. Garnish with fresh oregano, if desired.Makes 4 servings.

Nutrition information per serving: 190 calories, 21 g protein, 8 g carbohydrate, 10 g fat (1 g saturated), 53 mg cholesterol, 306 mg sodium, 594 mg potassium.

FISH KABOBS WITH CORIANDER RICE

If you'd rather grill these spicy kabobs, cook them on a greased rack over medium-hot coals for 8 to 12 minutes and turn often.

1½ pounds fresh *or* frozen halibut *or* sea
       bass steaks (1 inch thick)
¼   cup water
¼   cup lime juice
2   tablespoons olive oil *or* cooking oil
3   tablespoons snipped fresh parsley *or*
       1 teaspoon dried parsley flakes
1   clove garlic, minced
1   teaspoon ground cumin
     Dash pepper
3   small zucchini *and/or* yellow summer
       squash, cut into ¾-inch slices
       (3 cups)
1   large red sweet pepper, cut into ¾-inch
       pieces
2   cups water
2   cloves garlic, minced
2   teaspoons ground coriander
1   teaspoon ground cumin
½   teaspoon salt
⅛   teaspoon crushed red pepper
1   cup long grain rice
⅓   cup sliced pitted ripe olives
1   to 2 green onions, sliced
       (3 tablespoons)
     Lime slices, halved (optional)
     Thin red sweet pepper strips
       (optional)

Thaw fish, if frozen. Rinse fish. Cut fish into 1-inch cubes. Place in a plastic bag and set the bag into a bowl. Set aside.

In a small bowl combine ¼ cup water, lime juice, oil, parsley, 1 clove garlic, 1 teaspoon cumin, and pepper. Pour over fish. Close bag. Marinate for 30 minutes at room temperature, turning occasionally.

Meanwhile, cook zucchini or summer sqaush and sweet pepper pieces in a small amount of boiling water for 2 to 3 minutes or just till crisp-tender. Drain; set aside.

For coriander rice, in a medium saucepan combine 2 cups water, 2 cloves garlic, coriander, 1 teaspoon cumin, salt, and crushed red pepper. Bring to boiling; stir in the rice. Simmer, covered, for 15 minutes. Remove from heat; let stand, covered, for 5 minutes or till liquid is absorbed. Stir in olives and green onion.

While rice is cooking, drain fish, reserving marinade. Alternately thread fish, zucchini or summer squash, and sweet pepper pieces onto 6 long skewers. Brush with reserved marinade.

Place kabobs on the greased rack of an unheated broiler pan. Broil 3 to 4 inches from the heat for 6 to 10 minutes or till fish flakes easily with a fork, turning once. Serve kabobs with rice. Garnish with lime slices and red pepper strips, if desired. Makes 6 servings.

Nutrition information per serving: 311 calories, 27 g protein, 31 g carbohydrate, 9 g fat (1 g saturated), 36 mg cholesterol, 285 mg sodium, 759 mg potassium.

SPINACH-TOPPED SALMON

Salmon and asparagus are natural partners, so add some lightly steamed spears for a tasty side dish.

1½   pounds fresh *or* frozen salmon fillets
     (about ½ inch thick)
1   10-ounce package frozen chopped
     spinach, thawed
1   beaten egg
1   8-ounce container soft-style cream
     cheese with chives and onion
¼   cup grated Parmesan cheese
¾   cup herb-seasoned stuffing mix
2   tablespoons milk
2   tablespoons dry white wine *or* milk
¼   teaspoon garlic salt

Thaw fish, if frozen. Cut into 6 serving-size portions. Rinse fish; pat dry with paper towels. Place fish in a shallow baking dish; set aside.

For topping, drain spinach, pressing out excess liquid. In a small bowl combine egg, *half* of the cream cheese, and the Parmesan cheese. Stir in drained spinach and stuffing mix. Spoon *one-fourth* of the topping over *each* fillet. Bake, covered, in a 350° oven for 20 to 25 minutes or till fish flakes easily with a fork.

Meanwhile, for sauce, in a small saucepan combine remaining cream cheese, the milk, wine, and garlic salt. Cook and stir until cheese melts and mixture is smooth. Serve sauce over fish. Makes 6 servings.

Nutrition information per serving: 310 calories, 24 g protein, 10 g carbohydrate, 18 g fat (9 g saturated), 99 mg cholesterol, 543 mg sodium, 353 mg potassium.

HALIBUT À LA GRECO

It's the feta cheese, ripe olives, and pine nuts that add the exotic "Greco" or Greek flavor to halibut steaks.

1½ pounds fresh *or* frozen halibut steaks
   (¾ inch thick)
2 tablespoons margarine *or* butter
1 beaten egg
⅓ cup half-and-half, light cream, *or* milk
1 cup crumbled feta cheese
⅛ teaspoon ground red pepper
1 large tomato, chopped (1 cup)
¼ cup chopped pitted ripe olives
¼ cup pine nuts *or* slivered almonds,
   toasted
1 tablespoon lemon juice
   Lemon slices (optional)
   Fresh parsley sprigs (optional)

Thaw fish, if frozen. Cut fish into 6 serving-size portions. Rinse fish; pat dry with paper towels.

In a large skillet cook the fish in margarine or butter over medium-high heat for 3 minutes on each side (fish will be partially cooked). Transfer fish to a 2-quart rectangular baking dish; set aside.

In a small bowl stir together the egg and half and half, light cream or milk. Stir in the feta cheese and ground red pepper. Spoon mixture over fish. Sprinkle with tomato, olives, and pine nuts or almonds.

Bake, uncovered, in a 400° oven about 10 minutes or till fish flakes easily with a fork. Sprinkle fish with lemon juice. Transfer fish to dinner plates. Garnish with lemon slices and fresh parsley sprigs, if desired. Makes 6 servings.

Nutrition information per serving: 346 calories, 33 g protein, 5 g carbohydrate, 22 g fat (9 g saturated), 115 mg cholesterol, 623 mg sodium, 671 mg potassium.

LEMONY SCAMPI KABOBS

To peel and devein the shrimp, use your fingers to open and peel the shell down the body to the base of the tail. Using a sharp knife, make a shallow slit along the center of the back from the head end to the base of the tail. With the knife, remove the black sand vein.

1 pound fresh *or* frozen large shrimp
   in shells
2 small zucchini, cut into ¾-inch slices
   (2 cups)
1 large red sweet pepper, cut into 1-inch
   pieces (about 1½ cups)
1 clove garlic, minced
2 tablespoons margarine *or* butter
1 teaspoon finely shredded lemon peel
2 tablespoons lemon juice
¼ teaspoon ground red pepper
⅛ teaspoon salt
   Lemon wedges (optional)

Thaw shrimp, if frozen.

Peel shrimp leaving tail intact. Devein shrimp; rinse and pat dry. Set aside.

Cook zucchini in a small amount of lightly salted boiling water for 2 minutes; drain. On eight 12-inch skewers, alternately thread shrimp, zucchini, and red sweet pepper.

In a small saucepan cook garlic in margarine or butter. Stir in lemon peel, lemon juice, ground red pepper, and salt. Set aside.

Grill kabobs directly over hot coals for 5 minutes. Brush kabobs with lemon mixture. Turn kabobs and brush again. Grill for 3 to 7 minutes more or till shrimp turn pink. Serve with lemon wedges, if desired. Makes 4 servings.

Nutrition information per serving: 134 calories, 15 g protein, 4 g carbohydrate, 7 g fat (1 g saturated), 131 mg cholesterol, 285 mg sodium, 294 mg potassium.

SEA SHELL SCALLOPS

If you do not have coquille shells, use four individual au gratin dishes. Bake the scallops in a 450° oven for 10 to 12 minutes or till opaque. Top the scallops with the sauce and sprinkle with the crumb mixture. Bake for 3 minutes more or till crumbs are golden.

1 pound fresh *or* frozen scallops
1 10-ounce package frozen chopped
    spinach
¼ cup finely shredded carrot
2 green onions, thinly sliced (about
    2 tablespoons)
2 tablespoons margarine *or* butter
3 tablespoons all-purpose flour
¼ teaspoon dried tarragon, crushed
    Dash pepper
1 cup chicken *or* vegetable broth
⅓ cup half-and-half, light cream, *or* milk
¼ cup fine dry bread crumbs
2 tablespoons grated Parmesan cheese
2 tablespoons margarine *or* butter,
    melted
    Shredded carrot (optional)

Thaw scallops and spinach, if frozen. Cut any large scallops in half; set aside.

Drain spinach well; divide evenly among 4 coquille shells. Arrange scallops in a single layer on spinach. Broil 3 to 4 inches from the heat for 6 to 7 minutes or till scallops are opaque.

Meanwhile, for sauce, in a small saucepan cook the ¼ cup carrot and green onion in 2 tablespoons margarine or butter. Cook for 1 minute. Stir in flour, tarragon, and pepper. Add broth and half-and-half, light cream, or milk all at once. Cook and stir till mixture is thickened and bubbly. Cook and stir for 1 minute more. Spoon sauce over the scallops in shells.

In a small mixing bowl combine bread crumbs, Parmesan cheese and the 2 tablespoons melted margarine or butter; sprinkle over scallops and sauce in shells. Return to broiler; broil about 2 minutes or till crumbs are golden. Sprinkle with additional shredded carrot, if desired. Makes 4 servings.

Nutrition information per serving: 286 calories, 21 g protein, 15 g carbohydrate, 16 g fat (4 g saturated), 44 mg cholesterol, 656 mg sodium, 576 mg potassium.

SEAFOOD ENCHILADAS

Seafood-flavored fish, also known as Surimi, is made commercially by processing and re-forming minced fish to look like shellfish. It's a less expensive than crab or lobster, and as an added bonus, is lower in cholesterol.

12	ounces frozen, crab-flavored, salad-style fish
8	6¼-inch corn tortillas
1	medium red onion, finely chopped (½ cup)
2	cloves garlic, minced
1	teaspoon ground coriander
¼	teaspoon pepper
2	tablespoons margarine *or* butter
3	tablespoons all-purpose flour
1	8-ounce carton dairy sour cream
1	14½-ounce can chicken broth
1	*or* 2 canned jalapeño peppers, rinsed, seeded, and chopped *or* one 4-ounce can diced green chili peppers, drained
1	cup shredded Monterey Jack cheese (4 ounces)
	Chopped tomatoes (optional)
	Chopped red onion or sliced green onions (optional)
	Fresh cilantro (optional)

Thaw fish, if frozen. Flake coarsely; set aside.

Wrap corn tortillas in foil; place in a 350° oven for 10 to 15 minutes or till softened.

Meanwhile, for sauce, in a medium saucepan cook red onion, garlic, coriander, and pepper in margarine or butter till onion is tender. In a medium bowl stir flour into sour cream. Add broth; stir till combined. Add sour cream mixture to onion mixture. Stir in jalapeño or chili peppers. Cook and stir over medium heat till mixture is slightly thickened and bubbly. Remove from heat. Add *half* of the cheese; stir till melted.

For filling, stir ½ *cup* of the sauce into flaked fish. Place about ¼ *cup* of the filling on *each* tortilla; roll up. Arrange tortilla rolls, seam side down, in a lightly greased 2-quart rectangular baking dish. Top with remaining sauce. Bake, covered, in a 350° oven for 30 to 35 minutes or till heated through.

Sprinkle with remaining cheese. Bake, uncovered, about 5 minutes more or until cheese melts. Let stand for 10 minutes before serving. If desired, garnish with tomatoes, red or green onion, and cilantro. Makes 4 servings.

Nutrition information per serving: 550 calories, 26 g protein, 44 g carbohydrate, 30 g fat (15 g saturated), 68 mg cholesterol, 1,461 mg sodium, 439 mg potassium.

STEAMED MUSSELS VINAIGRETTE

Buy a few extra mussels to allow for those that don't open during cooking. Those that don't open are not suitable for eating.

1 pound mussels, scrubbed
3 quarts cold water
6 tablespoons salt
1 medium green pepper, finely chopped (½ cup)
3 cloves garlic, minced
2 tablespoons margarine *or* butter
1 medium tomato, seeded and chopped
½ cup dry white wine
2 tablespoons snipped fresh basil *or* 1 teaspoon dried basil, crushed
  Fresh basil (optional)
  French bread (optional)

Remove beards from mussels.

In a large bowl or kettle combine *1 quart* of the cold water and *2 tablespoons* of the salt; add mussels. Soak the mussels for 15 minutes; drain and rinse mussels. Discard soaking water. Repeat the soaking, draining, and rinsing process two more times.

In a 3-quart saucepan cook green pepper and garlic in margarine or butter till just crisp-tender. Stir in tomato, wine, and basil. Add mussels. Bring mixture to boiling; reduce heat. Cover and simmer for 3 to 4 minutes or just till mussels open. Remove from heat. Using a slotted spoon, remove mussels. (Discard any mussels that do not open.) Cover mussels and keep warm.

If necessary, simmer the sauce, uncovered, until it has been reduced to 1 cup. Pour the sauce over the mussels. Garnish with fresh basil and serve with French bread, if desired. Makes 2 main-dish servings or 4 appetizer servings.

Nutrition information per serving: 295 calories, 15 g protein, 26 g carbohydrate, 11 g fat (2 g saturated), 27 mg cholesterol, 818 mg sodium, 344 mg potassium.

PEPPER SHRIMP IN PEANUT SAUCE

Save time by buying 12 ounces of cooked, peeled, and deveined shrimp.

1   pound fresh *or* frozen shrimp in shells
8   ounces farfalle (bow-tie pasta) *or*
    linguine *or* 1 cup long-grain rice
½   cup water
¼   cup orange marmalade
2   tablespoons peanut butter
2   tablespoons soy sauce
2   teaspoons cornstarch
¼   teaspoon crushed red pepper
1   tablespoon cooking oil
2   medium red, yellow, *and/or* green
    sweet peppers, cut into strips
    (about 2½ cups)
6   green onions, bias-sliced into 1-inch
    pieces
    Chopped peanuts (optional)

Thaw shrimp, if frozen. Peel and devein shrimp; rinse and pat dry. Set aside.

Cook pasta or rice according to package directions; drain.

Meanwhile, for sauce, in a small bowl stir together water, orange marmalade, peanut butter, soy sauce, cornstarch, and crushed red pepper. Set aside.

Pour cooking oil into a wok or large skillet. (Add more oil as necessary during cooking.) Preheat on medium-high heat. Add pepper strips and green onions; stir-fry for 1 to 2 minutes or till crisp-tender. Remove and set aside.

Add *half* of the shrimp to wok; stir-fry 2 to 3 minutes or till shrimp turn pink; remove and set aside. Repeat with the remaining shrimp.

Stir sauce; add to center of wok. Cook and stir till thickened and bubbly. Cook and stir for 2 minutes more. Remove from heat; keep sauce warm.

In a 4-quart Dutch oven or kettle combine cooked pasta or rice, vegetable mixture, and shrimp; cook over medium heat till heated through, tossing gently to mix. Serve shrimp mixture on dinner plates. Top with sauce. If desired, sprinkle with chopped peanuts. Makes 4 servings.

Nutrition information per serving: 435 calories, 24 g protein, 64 g carbohydrate, 9 g fat (2 g saturated), 131 mg cholesterol, 710 mg sodium, 336 mg potassium.

SCALLOPS WITH ARUGULA

Splurge! In less than 30 minutes, you can create an impressive entrée of sweet scallops topped with a rich, creamy tomato sauce.

1 pound fresh *or* frozen bay *or* sea
    scallops
3 large yellow *and/or* red sweet peppers
2 tablespoons margarine *or* butter
1 clove garlic, minced
4 cups torn arugula *or* spinach
    (2 ounces)
½ cup whipping cream
2 tablespoons tomato paste
2 tablespoons lime juice
¼ teaspoon salt
¼ teaspoon pepper

Thaw scallops, if frozen. Rinse and pat dry. Cut any large scallops in half. Set aside.

Slice peppers lengthwise into ½-inch-wide strips.

In a large skillet melt the margarine or butter over medium-high heat. Stir-fry the sweet pepper strips and garlic for 4 to 5 minutes or till just tender. Add arugula or spinach; stir-fry for 30 seconds or till just wilted. Divide vegetable mixture among four dinner plates. Cover; keep warm.

To the same skillet add cream and tomato paste. Bring mixture to boiling; add scallops. Simmer, uncovered, for 3 to 4 minutes or till scallops are opaque. Remove scallops with a slotted spoon; arrange scallops alongside vegetables.

Return cream mixture to boiling; cook for 1 minute or till mixture is slightly thickened, stirring briskly with a whisk. Add lime juice, salt, and pepper. Spoon cream mixture over scallops. Makes 4 servings.

Nutrition information per serving: 260 calories, 17 g protein, 9 g carbohydrate, 18 g fat (8 g saturated), 75 mg cholesterol, 453 mg sodium, 613 mg potassium.

LOBSTER AND ASPARAGUS ALFREDO

One fresh or frozen lobster tail weighing 10 to 12 ounces yields just the right amount of cooked meat for this richly sauced pasta dish.

8 ounces fettuccine
1 cup asparagus cut into 1-inch pieces
    or broccoli flowerets
1 cup sliced fresh mushrooms
2 tablespoons margarine *or* butter
6 ounces cooked lobster meat, cut into
    bite-size pieces (about 1¼ cups)
⅔ cup half-and-half *or* light cream
¾ cup shredded Parmesan cheese
    (3 ounces)
⅛ teaspoon coarsely ground black
    pepper
   Dash ground nutmeg
   Coarsely ground black pepper
    (optional)
   Breadsticks (optional)

Cook fettuccine according to package directions; drain. Set aside.

Meanwhile, in a large skillet cook asparagus or broccoli and mushrooms in margarine or butter for 5 minutes or till just tender. Add lobster and half-and-half or light cream; heat through.

Add cooked fettuccine to the skillet. Then add Parmesan cheese, ⅛ teaspoon pepper, and nutmeg. Toss till pasta is coated. If necessary, cook for 2 to 3 minutes till sauce is desired consistency. Serve immediately. Sprinkle with additional pepper and serve with breadsticks, if desired. Makes 4 servings.

Nutrition information per serving: 468 calories, 26 g protein, 50 g carbohydrate, 18 g fat (8 g saturated), 60 mg cholesterol, 597 mg sodium, 390 mg potassium.

CRAB MORNAY

A combination of natural and processed Swiss cheese makes the sauce extra smooth and creamy.

1   to 1¼ pounds fresh *or* frozen cooked
    crab legs (1½ cups cooked
    crabmeat)
1   10-ounce package (6) frozen patty
    shells
1   cup sliced fresh mushrooms
1   small leek, sliced, *or* ⅓ cup sliced green
    onion
1   clove garlic, minced
2   tablespoons margarine *or* butter
2   tablespoons all-purpose flour
    Dash white pepper
2   cups half and half, light cream, *or*
    milk
½   cup shredded Swiss cheese (2 ounces)
½   cup shredded process Swiss cheese
    (2 ounces)
2   tablespoons dry sherry
    Fresh chives (optional)
    Fresh thyme (optional)

Thaw crab, if frozen. (Ask your butcher to crack fresh crab legs for you. Otherwise, use kitchen shears to crack them open.) Remove crabmeat from shells and cut up. Set aside.

Bake patty shells according to package directions.

In a medium saucepan cook mushrooms, leek or green onions, and garlic in margarine or butter till tender, but not brown. Stir in flour, and white pepper. Add half and half, light cream, or milk all at once. Cook and stir till mixture is thickened and bubbly; cook and stir for 1 minute more. Reduce heat.

Add natural Swiss cheese and process Swiss cheese to cream mixture; stir till melted. Stir in crabmeat and dry sherry. Heat through; *do not* boil. Serve immediately in patty shells. Garnish with fresh chives and thyme, if desired. Makes 6 servings.

Nutrition information per serving: 483 calories, 17 g protein, 27 g carbohydrate, 34 g fat (10 g saturated), 80 mg cholesterol, 510 mg sodium, 335 mg potassium.

SEAFOOD LASAGNA

Treat yourself to a version of lasagna that's even more indulgent than the traditional one.

1   8-ounce package frozen crab-flavored
       fish pieces
½   cup frozen, peeled, cooked shrimp *or*
       one 4½-ounce can shrimp, drained
2   14- *or* 16-ounce cans stewed
       tomatoes, cut up
½   cup sliced fresh mushrooms
½   teaspoon onion powder
½   teaspoon dried oregano, crushed
       Dash salt
       Dash pepper
3   tablespoons margarine *or* butter
3   tablespoons all-purpose flour
1¾ cups milk
1   cup shredded Swiss cheese (4 ounces)
¼   cup dry white wine
8   lasagna noodles, cooked
¼   cup grated Romano *or* Parmesan
       cheese
       Fresh oregano (optional)

Thaw crab-flavored fish and shrimp, if frozen. Cut or flake fish into bite-size pieces; set fish and shrimp aside.

For shrimp sauce, in a medium saucepan combine *undrained* tomatoes, mushrooms, onion powder, oregano, salt, and pepper. Bring to boiling; reduce heat. Simmer, uncovered, about 20 minutes or till mixture is thickened. Remove from heat. Stir in shrimp. Set aside.

For cheese sauce, in a medium saucepan melt margarine or butter. Stir in flour. Add milk all at once. Cook and stir over medium heat till thickened and bubbly. Cook and stir for 1 minute more. Add Swiss cheese; stir till melted. Stir in crab-flavored fish and wine.

In an 11x7x1½-inch baking dish, layer *half* of the shrimp sauce, *half* of the lasagna noodles, and *half* of the cheese sauce. Repeat layers. Sprinkle with Romano or Parmesan cheese. Bake, uncovered, in a 350° oven for 25 minutes or till heated through. Let stand for 15 minutes before serving. Garnish with fresh oregano, if desired. Makes 6 to 8 servings.

Nutrition information per serving: 347 calories, 20 g protein, 33 g carbohydrate, 15 g fat (6 g saturated), 58 mg cholesterol, 925 mg sodium, 566 mg potassium.

SPINACH FETTUCCINE WITH MUSHROOM CLAM SAUCE

Making your own spinach fettuccine is fun, if you have the time, and tastes even better than refrigerated pasta. If you haven't got the time and you can't find refrigerated variety, use half the amount of dried pasta.

8   ounces refrigerated spinach *or* plain
      fettuccine
2   6½-ounce cans chopped *or* minced
      clams
      Half-and-half, light cream, *or* milk
1   cup sliced fresh mushrooms
4   green onions, sliced (½ cup)
2   cloves garlic, minced
2   tablespoons margarine *or* butter
¼   cup all-purpose flour
1   tablespoon snipped fresh basil *or*
      1 teaspoon dried basil, crushed
1½ teaspoons snipped fresh oregano *or*
      teaspoon dried oregano, crushed
⅛   teaspoon pepper
¼   cup snipped parsley
¼   cup dry white wine, half-and-half,
      light cream, *or* milk
¼   cup shredded Parmesan cheese
      Fresh basil (optional)

Cook fettuccine according to package directions; drain well. Set fettuccine aside.

Meanwhile, drain clams, reserving liquid from *one* of the cans. Add enough half-and-half, light cream, or milk to the reserved liquid to make 1½ cups.

For sauce, in a medium saucepan cook mushrooms, green onions, and garlic in margarine or butter till tender. Stir in flour, basil, oregano, and pepper; add clam juice mixture all at once. Cook and stir till thickened and bubbly. Cook and stir for 1 minute more. Stir in clams, parsley, and the ¼ cup wine, half-and-half, light cream, or milk; heat through.

Divide fettuccine among four dinner plates. Spoon clam sauce over each. Sprinkle with Parmesan cheese. Garnish with additional fresh basil, if desired. Makes 4 servings.

Nutrition information per serving: 310 calories, 16 g protein, 32 g carbohydrate, 13 g fat (4 g saturated), 74 mg cholesterol, 221 mg sodium, 348 mg potassium.

SHRIMP WITH PEPPERS AND CORN

Because jalapeño peppers contain volatile oils that can burn your skin and eyes, avoid direct contact with the peppers. When seeding and chopping them wear plastic or rubber gloves or work under cold running water. If your bare hands touch the peppers, wash them well with soap and water.

1½ pounds fresh *or* frozen peeled, deveined medium *or* jumbo shrimp
1 cup water
1 teaspoon instant chicken bouillon granules
2 cups fresh corn *or* frozen corn, thawed
1 large red *or* green sweet pepper, chopped (1 cup)
2 to 4 cloves garlic, minced
1 tablespoon cooking oil
¼ cup dry white wine
2 tablespoons lemon juice
1 teaspoon cornstarch
1 fresh jalapeño pepper, seeded and finely chopped
½ teaspoon dried oregano, crushed
¼ teaspoon salt
⅛ to ¼ teaspoon ground red pepper
⅛ teaspoon ground cumin
Fresh whole jalapeño peppers (optional)

Thaw shrimp, if frozen. Rinse shrimp; set aside.

In a 10-inch skillet combine water and chicken bouillon granules. Bring to boiling. Add shrimp; return to boiling. Reduce heat; cover and simmer for 1 to 3 minutes or till shrimp turn pink. Drain shrimp in a colander; set aside.

In the same skillet cook corn, red or green sweet pepper, and garlic in hot oil for 3 minutes or till corn is tender, stirring often. Set aside.

In a small bowl stir together white wine, lemon juice, cornstarch, finely chopped jalapeño pepper, oregano, salt, ground red pepper, and cumin. Stir the wine mixture into the vegetable mixture in the skillet. Cook and stir till the mixture is thickened and bubbly.

Return drained shrimp to skillet. Cook for 2 minutes more or till mixture is heated through, stirring gently. Garnish with whole jalapeño peppers, if desired. Makes 4 to 6 servings.

Nutrition information per serving: 272 calories, 31 g protein, 23 g carbohydrate, 6 g fat (1 g saturated), 261 mg cholesterol, 501 mg sodium, 524 mg potassium.

CRAB, LOBSTER, AND SHRIMP NEWBURG

To cut the cost without sacrificing flavor, use crab- and lobster-flavored fish instead of the seafood in this rich and saucy main course.

4 ounces frozen, peeled, cooked shrimp (about ½ cup)
2 tablespoons margarine *or* butter
2 tablespoons all-purpose flour
¼ teaspoon salt
    Dash ground red pepper
1¼ cups milk
1 egg yolk, beaten
1 6- *or* 7-ounce can crabmeat, drained, flaked, and cartilage removed, *or* 7 ounces cooked crabmeat (about 1½ cups)
3 ounces cooked lobster, cut into bite-size pieces (about 1 cup)
3 tablespoons Madeira *or* dry sherry
4 baked patty shells *or* 2 cups hot cooked rice *or* pasta
    Fresh sage (optional)

Thaw shrimp, if frozen; set aside.

In a medium saucepan melt margarine or butter. Stir in flour, salt, and red pepper. Add milk all at once. Cook and stir till mixture is thickened and bubbly. Cook and stir for 1 minute more.

Stir about *half* of the hot mixture into the egg yolk. Return all of the egg mixture to the saucepan. Cook and stir just till mixture bubbles. Reduce heat. Cook and stir for 2 minutes more.

Stir in shrimp, crabmeat, lobster, and Madeira or sherry; heat through. Spoon into patty shells or serve over hot cooked rice or pasta. If desired, garnish with sage. Makes 4 servings.

Nutrition information per serving: 453 calories, 26 g protein, 26 g carbohydrate, 26 g fat (3 g saturated), 182 mg cholesterol, 833 mg sodium, 369 mg potassium.

PASTA WITH SCALLOPS AND FRESH VEGETABLES

When sugar snap peas are out of season, switch to fresh Chinese pea pods, cut in half crosswise.

1 pound fresh *or* frozen sea scallops
8 ounces fettuccine *or* linguine
1 tablespoon margarine *or* butter
1 tablespoon cooking oil
2 to 3 cloves garlic, minced
2 large carrots, thinly bias sliced (about 1½ cups)
6 ounces sugar snap peas (2 cups)
3 green onions, thinly sliced (¼ cup)
½ cup dry white wine
⅓ cup water
1 tablespoon snipped fresh dill *or* 2 teaspoons snipped fresh tarragon
1 teaspoon instant chicken bouillon granules
¼ teaspoon crushed red pepper
2 tablespoons cornstarch
2 tablespoons cold water
¼ cup grated Parmesan cheese
Cracked black pepper

Thaw scallops, if frozen. Cut any large scallops in half; set aside.

In a Dutch oven cook pasta according to package directions; drain. Return pasta to Dutch oven; toss with margarine or butter. Cover to keep warm.

Meanwhile, pour oil into a wok or large skillet. Heat over medium-high heat. Add garlic; stir-fry garlic for 15 seconds. Add carrots; stir-fry for 4 minutes. Add sugar snap peas and green onions; stir-fry for 2 to 3 minutes more or till all of the vegetables are crisp-tender. Remove vegetables from the wok. Cool wok for 1 minute.

Carefully add wine, the ⅓ cup water, dill or tarragon, bouillon granules, and crushed red pepper to wok. Bring to boiling. Add scallops; reduce heat. Simmer, uncovered, for 1 to 2 minutes or till scallops are opaque, stirring occasionally.

Stir together cornstarch and the 2 tablespoons cold water; add to wok. Cook and stir till mixture is thickened and bubbly. Return vegetables to wok; add pasta. Toss to mix all ingredients together. Heat through. Transfer to dinner plates. Sprinkle with cracked black pepper. Makes 4 servings.

Nutrition information per serving: 462 calories, 27 g protein, 60 g carbohydrate, 10 g fat (2 g saturated), 39 mg cholesterol, 577 mg sodium, 621 mg potassium.

SEAFOOD ARTICHOKE PIZZA

Toasted walnuts add a wonderfully rich flavor to seafood. To toast walnuts, spread nuts in a thin layer in a shallow baking pan. Bake at 350° for 5 to 10 minutes or till golden, stirring once or twice.

8   ounces fresh *or* frozen, peeled, deveined medium shrimp
1   12-inch Italian bread shell (16 ounces)
4   cups water
½   cup soft-style *or* whipped cream cheese with smoked salmon
½   cup shredded Swiss cheese (2 ounces)
⅓   cup dairy sour cream
1   6½-ounce jar marinated artichoke hearts, drained and thinly sliced
4   ounces thinly sliced, smoked salmon (lox-style), cut into strips (optional)
1   small tomato, chopped (½ cup)
½   medium green pepper, chopped (½ cup)
2   tablespoons chopped walnuts, toasted

Thaw shrimp, if frozen.

Bake Italian bread shell in a 450° oven for 8 to 10 minutes or till heated through.

Meanwhile, rinse shrimp under cold running water. In a medium saucepan combine shrimp and water. Bring to boiling. Reduce heat. Simmer, uncovered, for 1 to 3 minutes or till shrimp turn pink, stirring occasionally. Drain shrimp. Rinse under cold running water; drain again. Set aside.

Stir together cream cheese, Swiss cheese, and sour cream. Spread warm Italian bread shell with the cream cheese mixture. Arrange shrimp, artichoke hearts, salmon (if desired), tomato, and green pepper on top of the cream cheese mixture. Sprinkle with walnuts. Makes 4 servings.

Nutrition information per serving: 395 calories, 20 g protein, 38 g carbohydrate, 19 g fat (7 g saturated), 92 mg cholesterol, 720 mg sodium, 220 mg potassium.

CRAWFISH JAMBALAYA

Jambalaya (jam-ba-LIE-ya) is a hearty Cajun rice dish. The name comes from the French word for ham, jambon, but Cajun cooks often add crawfish and seafood.

12	ounces fresh *or* frozen, peeled, cooked crawfish *or* peeled, deveined, cooked shrimp
2	stalks celery, sliced (1 cup)
1	large onion, chopped (1 cup)
1	medium green pepper, chopped (1 cup)
1	clove garlic, minced
2	tablespoons margarine *or* butter
1⅔	cups water
½	teaspoon salt
½	teaspoon dried thyme, crushed
⅛	to ¼ teaspoon crushed red pepper
⅛	teaspoon ground black pepper
1	bay leaf
½	cup long grain rice
1	16-ounce can tomatoes, cut up
½	of a 6-ounce can tomato paste
	Celery leaves (optional)

Thaw crawfish or shrimp, if frozen. Rinse crawfish or shrimp under cold running water; set aside.

In a 3-quart saucepan cook celery, onion, green pepper, and garlic in margarine or butter about 5 minutes or till tender. Add water, salt, thyme, red pepper, black pepper, and bay leaf. Bring mixture to boiling. Add rice. Reduce heat; cover and simmer for 15 minutes or till rice is tender.

Stir in *undrained* tomatoes and tomato paste. Add crawfish or shrimp. Cook for 2 to 3 minutes more or till crawfish or shrimp are heated through. Remove bay leaf. Serve in soup bowls. Garnish with celery leaves, if desired. Makes 4 servings.

Nutrition information per serving: 296 calories, 23 g protein, 36 g carbohydrate, 7 g fat (1 g saturated), 166 mg cholesterol, 935 mg sodium, 903 mg potassium.

CHEESY GRILLED LOBSTER TAILS

Unlike Maine lobsters which have large, meaty claws, most of the meat in rock or "spiny" lobsters is found in the tail.

4 medium fresh *or* frozen rock lobster
    tails (5 ounces each)
3 tablespoons margarine *or* butter
3 to 4 green onions, sliced (¼ cup)
1 clove garlic, minced
1½ cups soft bread crumbs (2 slices)
¾ cup shredded creamy havarti cheese
    (3 ounces)
2 teaspoons snipped fresh basil *or*
    ½ teaspoon dried basil, crushed
2 tablespoons margarine *or* butter,
    melted

Thaw lobster tails, if frozen.

Rinse lobster tails; pat dry with paper towels. To butterfly tails, cut lengthwise through centers of hard top shells and meat, using kitchen shear or a sharp heavy knife. Cut to, but not through, the bottom shells. Using fingers, spread meat apart slightly.

For stuffing, in a medium skillet melt the 3 tablespoons margarine or butter. Add green onions and garlic. Cook for 1 minute; remove skillet from heat. Stir in bread crumbs. Then stir in cheese and basil; toss to mix. Spoon stuffing into slits in lobster tails.

Arrange medium-hot coals around edges of grill; place a drip pan in center of grill. Test for medium heat over the drip pan. Place lobster tails over drip pan, stuffing side up. Cover and grill for 25 to 30 minutes or till lobster meat is opaque. Drizzle lobster tails with 2 tablespoons melted margarine or butter. Makes 4 servings.

Broiler method: Prepare lobster and stuffing as directed above *except* do not stuff lobster tails. Place unstuffed lobster tails on the unheated rack of a broiler pan. Broil lobster 4 to 6 inches from the heat for 10 to 11 minutes or till meat is opaque. Spoon stuffing into slits in lobster tails. Broil for 1 to 2 minutes more or till stuffing is light brown and heated through.

Nutrition information per serving: 355 calories, 25 g protein, 11 g carbohydrate, 24 g fat (3 g saturated), 91 mg cholesterol, 704 mg sodium, 377 mg potassium.

SCALLOPS WITH MUSTARD SAUCE

For a fuller, more piquant flavor use a tarragon-flavored mustard.

12 ounces fresh *or* frozen sea scallops
½ cup chicken *or* vegetable broth
2 tablespoons Dijon-style *or* herbed
   mustard
2 tablespoons white wine
   Worcestershire sauce
1 tablespoon cornstarch
   Dash white pepper
2 tablespoons cooking oil
1 small zucchini, cut into julienne strips
   (1 cup)
1 small yellow summer squash, cut into
   julienne strips (1 cup)
4 green onions, bias sliced into 1-inch
   pieces (about ¼ cup)
6 ounces fusilli *or* spaghetti, cooked and
   drained
2 tablespoons cashews *or* peanuts
4 cherry tomatoes, halved (optional)

Thaw scallops, if frozen. Rinse scallops; pat dry with paper towels. Cut any large scallops in half; set aside.

For sauce, in a small bowl combine chicken or vegetable broth, mustard, Worcestershire sauce, cornstarch, and white pepper; set aside.

In a wok or large skillet heat oil over medium-high heat. Add zucchini, yellow squash, and green onions; stir fry for 2 to 3 minutes or till crisp tender. Remove vegetables from wok or skillet.

Add scallops to wok or skillet; stir-fry for 2 to 3 minutes or till scallops are opaque; remove scallops. Stir sauce; add to wok or skillet. Cook and stir till mixture is thickened and bubbly.

Return vegetables and scallops to skillet; heat through. Divide pasta among four dinner plates. Top with scallop mixture. Sprinkle with cashews or peanuts. Garnish with cherry tomato halves, if desired. Makes 4 servings.

Nutrition information per serving: 343 calories, 19 g protein, 42 g carbohydrate, 11 g fat (2 g saturated), 26 mg cholesterol, 506 mg sodium, 462 mg potassium.

FLORIDA CRAB CAKES

Confused about whether the crabmeat you purchased is cooked? Relax, all crabmeat is sold cooked.

1   6-ounce package frozen crabmeat *or* one 6-ounce can crabmeat, drained, flaked and cartilage removed (about 1½ cups)
1   egg, slightly beaten
½   cup fine dry bread crumbs
2   green onions, finely chopped (2 tablespoons)
2   tablespoons mayonnaise *or* salad dressing
1   tablespoon snipped parsley
2   teaspoons snipped fresh thyme *or* ½ teaspoon dried thyme, crushed
2   teaspoons Dijon-style *or* Creole mustard
½   teaspoon white wine Worcestershire sauce
⅛   teaspoon salt
¼   cup cornmeal
2   tablespoons cooking oil
    Salad greens (optional)
    Tartar sauce (optional)
    Lemon wedges (optional)

Thaw crab, if frozen; set aside.

In a medium bowl combine egg, *¼ cup* of the fine dry bread crumbs, green onions, mayonnaise or salad dressing, parsley, thyme, mustard, Worcestershire sauce, and salt. Add crab; mix well. Shape crab mixture into four ¾-inch-thick patties.

In a small bowl combine remaining fine dry bread crumbs and cornmeal. Coat patties with cornmeal mixture.

In a large skillet heat the cooking oil; add crab cakes. Cook over medium heat about 3 minutes on each side or till crab cakes are golden and heated through, adding additional oil, if necessary. Serve crab cakes on a bed of salad greens and top with tartar sauce, if desired. Garnish with lemon wedges, if desired. Makes 4 servings.

Tartar Sauce: In a small bowl stir together 1 cup *mayonnaise or salad dressing,* ¼ cup *finely chopped dill pickle or sweet pickle relish,* 1 tablespoon sliced *green onion,* 1 tablespoon snipped *parsley,* 1 tablespoon diced *pimiento,* and 1 teaspoon *lemon juice.* Cover and chill till serving. Makes 1 cup.

Nutrition information per serving: 259 calories, 13 g protein, 17 g carbohydrate, 15 g fat (2 g saturated), 100 mg cholesterol, 401 mg sodium, 216 mg potassium.

SHRIMP CURRY

Tease your taste buds with this invigorating alliance of sweet raisins and hot pepper sauce.

12	ounces fresh *or* frozen, peeled, deveined shrimp
1	large onion, chopped (1 cup)
1	medium green pepper, cut into 1-inch pieces (1 cup)
1	stalk celery, sliced (½ cup)
1	clove garlic, minced
2	tablespoons cooking oil
1	16-ounce can tomatoes, cut up
½	cup slivered almonds
½	cup raisins
¼	cup snipped parsley
¼	cup chili sauce
1	teaspoon lemon juice
½	teaspoon salt
½	teaspoon bottled hot pepper sauce
¼	teaspoon white pepper
¼	teaspoon curry powder
¼	teaspoon dried thyme, crushed
2	cups hot cooked rice
¼	cup slivered almonds, toasted

Thaw shrimp, if frozen. Rinse; pat dry with paper towels. Set aside.

In a 12-inch skillet cook onion, green pepper, celery, and garlic in hot oil till crisp-tender; add *undrained* tomatoes, ½ cup almonds, raisins, parsley, chili sauce, lemon juice, salt, bottled hot pepper sauce, white pepper, curry powder, and thyme. Bring mixture to boiling; reduce heat. Cover and simmer for 30 minutes.

Add shrimp to tomato mixture. Return to boiling; reduce heat. Cover and simmer about 5 minutes more or till shrimp turn pink. Serve over hot cooked rice. Sprinkle *each* serving with *1 tablespoon* toasted almonds. Makes 4 servings.

Nutrition information per serving: 511 calories, 24 g protein, 63 g carbohydrate, 20 g fat (2 g saturated), 131 mg cholesterol, 841 mg sodium, 972 mg potassium.

SNAPPER AND PASTA STEW

This full-flavored stew is packed with crisp, colorful vegetables, shell-shaped pasta, and chunks of fish—all mingling together in a lightly herbed broth.

1 pound fresh *or* frozen skinless red
    snapper *or* rockfish fillets
6 medium leeks, sliced (about 3 cups)
1 medium green sweet pepper, cut into
    strips (1 cup)
1 medium yellow *or* red sweet pepper,
    cut into strips (1 cup)
2 cloves garlic, minced
2 tablespoons cooking oil
1 16-ounce tomatoes, cut up
1¼ cups water
2 tablespoons snipped fresh basil *or*
    1 teaspoon dried basil, crushed
1 teaspoon snipped fresh rosemary *or*
    ¼ teaspoon dried rosemary, crushed
¼ teaspoon salt
¼ teaspoon pepper
1 cup medium shell macaroni
¼ cup sliced pitted ripe olives
    Fresh rosemary (optional)
    Sliced pitted ripe olives (optional)

Thaw fish, if frozen. Rinse fish. Cut into 1-inch cubes; set aside.

In a large saucepan cook leeks, green pepper, yellow or red pepper, and garlic in hot oil till vegetables are crisp-tender. Stir in *undrained* tomatoes, water, basil, rosemary, salt, and pepper. Bring mixture to boiling. Add shell macaroni. Reduce heat; cover and simmer about 15 minutes or till shells are tender.

Add fish and ¼ cup olives to tomato mixture; return to boiling. Reduce heat. Cover and simmer for 4 to 6 minutes or till fish flakes easily with a fork. Garnish with fresh rosemary and additional sliced olives, if desired. Makes 4 servings.

Nutrition information per serving: 359 calories, 29 g protein, 39 g carbohydrate, 11 g fat (2 g saturated), 42 mg cholesterol, 429 mg sodium, 969 mg potassium.

SEAFOOD STEW

Crispy slices of French bread are perfect for soaking up the last drop of this savory stew.

8 ounces skinless cusk (ocean catfish) *or* cod fillets, cut into ¾-inch pieces
8 fresh *or* frozen clams in shells
6 quarts water
9 tablespoons salt
2 medium potatoes, coarsely chopped (about 2 cups)
1 12-ounce can whole kernel corn with sweet peppers, drained
1 14½-ounce can stewed tomatoes
½ cup chicken *or* vegetable broth
1½ teaspoons snipped fresh thyme *or* ¼ teaspoon dried thyme, crushed
¼ teaspoon garlic powder
⅛ teaspoon pepper
1 tablespoon snipped fresh parsley *or* thyme

Thaw fish and clams, if frozen. Rinse fish. Cut fish into 1-inch pieces. Wash clams well. Set fish and clams aside.

In a large bowl combine *2 quarts* of the water and *3 tablespoons* of the salt; add clams. Let clams soak for 15 minutes; drain and rinse. Discard the soaking water. Repeat soaking, draining, and rinsing clams two more times with the remaining water and salt.

For stew, in a large saucepan or Dutch oven combine potatoes, corn, *undrained* tomatoes, chicken or vegetable broth, thyme, garlic powder, and pepper. Bring mixture to boiling; reduce heat. Cover and simmer for 10 minutes.

Add fish and clams. Cover and cook for 4 to 5 minutes or till fish flakes easily with a fork and clams open. Spoon into bowls. Sprinkle with fresh parsley or thyme. Makes 4 servings.

Nutrition information per serving: 231 calories, 19 g protein, 38 g carbohydrate, 2 g fat (0 g saturated), 37 mg cholesterol, 846 mg sodium, 872 mg potassium.

MONKFISH-ZUCCHINI CHOWDER

Cusk, or ocean catfish, is another low-fat fish with a mild flavor and firm-texture that you also could use in this creamy chowder.

1   pound fresh *or* frozen monkfish fillets
1   medium onion, chopped (½ cup)
2   tablespoons margarine *or* butter
3   small potatoes, peeled and sliced
        (about 2 cups)
1½   cups chicken broth
1   cup whole milk, half-and-half, *or* light
        cream
1   2-ounce jar diced pimiento, drained
2   tablespoons snipped parsley
¼   teaspoon dried thyme, crushed
     Dash pepper
2   small zucchini, sliced (about 2 cups)
     Salt
     Pepper
     Fresh thyme (optional)

Thaw fish, if frozen. Rinse fish. Cut into ¾-inch cubes; set aside.

In a large saucepan cook the onion in the margarine or butter till tender. Stir in potatoes and broth. Bring mixture to boiling; reduce heat. Cover and simmer about 25 minutes or till potatoes are very tender.

Place the broth mixture in a blender container or food processor bowl. Cover and blend or process till smooth.

Return mixture to saucepan. Stir in milk, half-and-half, or light cream; pimiento; parsley; thyme; and pepper. Bring to boiling; reduce heat. Add fish cubes. Cook for 5 minutes, stirring constantly to prevent scorching. Stir in zucchini. Cook and stir for 3 to 5 minutes more or till fish flakes easily with a fork. Season to taste with salt and pepper. Garnish with fresh thyme, if desired. Makes 4 servings.

Nutrition information per serving: 254 calories, 22 g protein, 18 g carbohydrate, 10 g fat (3 g saturated), 37 mg cholesterol, 414 mg sodium, 968 mg potassium..

CREAMY SHRIMP AND SPINACH STEW

A dash of nutmeg brings out the best in the shrimp and emphasizes the slightly sweet, nutty taste of the Gruyère cheese.

8 ounces fresh *or* frozen, peeled, deveined small shrimp
1 cup sliced fresh mushrooms
1 medium onion, chopped (½ cup)
1 clove garlic, minced
2 tablespoons margarine *or* butter
3 tablespoons all-purpose flour
1 bay leaf
⅛ teaspoon ground nutmeg
⅛ teaspoon pepper
1 14½-ounce can vegetable *or* chicken broth
1 cup half-and-half, light cream, *or* milk
2 cups torn fresh spinach
¾ cup shredded Gruyère cheese (3 ounces)

Thaw shrimp, if frozen. Rinse shrimp; set aside.

In a medium saucepan cook mushrooms, onion, and garlic in margarine or butter till tender. Stir in flour, bay leaf, nutmeg, and pepper. Add vegetable or chicken broth and half-and-half, light cream, or milk all at once. Cook and stir till mixture is thickened and bubbly.

Add shrimp. Cook for 2 minutes more. Add spinach and Gruyère cheese. Cook and stir till spinach wilts and cheese melts. Remove and discard bay leaf. Makes 4 servings.

Nutrition information per serving: 370 calories, 22 g protein, 22 g carbohydrate, 22 g fat (10 g saturated), 135 mg cholesterol, 965 mg sodium, 603 mg potassium.

FISH AND CORN CHOWDER

Sprinkle a few rye croutons over the chowder just before serving to add a bit of crunch and contrast to the sweetness of the corn.

12 ounces fresh *or* frozen skinless cod, cusk, haddock *or* pike fillets
¾ cup chicken *or* vegetable broth
1 medium carrot, shredded (½ cup)
½ stalk celery, chopped (¼ cup)
½ small green pepper, chopped (¼ cup)
1 17-ounce can cream-style corn
1 12-ounce can (1½ cups) evaporated milk
1 cup shredded process Swiss cheese (4 ounces)
Celery leaves (optional)

Thaw fish, if frozen. Rinse fish. Cut into ¾-inch pieces. Set aside.

In a medium saucepan combine chicken or vegetable broth, shredded carrot, chopped celery, and green pepper. Bring mixture to boiling; reduce heat. Cover and simmer for 2 minutes. Stir in corn and evaporated milk. Bring mixture to boiling, stirring occasionally.

Add fish; reduce heat. Cover and simmer gently for 3 to 5 minutes or till fish flakes easily with a fork. Gradually add cheese, stirring till melted. Garnish with celery leaves, if desired. Makes 4 servings.

Nutrition information per serving: 344 calories, 32 g protein, 35 g carbohydrate, 9 g fat (5 g saturated), 63 mg cholesterol, 733 mg sodium, 754 mg potassium.

SIMPLE SEAFOOD GUMBO

Ready-to-go products like Cajun-style stewed tomatoes and cooked seafood make everything simple and foolproof in this hearty gumbo.

1 medium green pepper, chopped
    (1 cup)
1 medium onion, chopped (½ cup)
1 tablespoon cooking oil
1 tablespoon cornstarch
1 14½-ounce can Cajun-style stewed
    tomatoes
2 6-ounce cans (1½ cups) hot-style
    tomato juice
½ of a 10-ounce package frozen sliced
    okra (1 cup)
1 8-ounce package frozen, peeled,
    cooked shrimp
½ of an 8-ounce package frozen, crab-
    flavored, salad-style fish (about
    1 cup)
¾ cup quick-cooking rice
½ cup beef broth

In a large saucepan cook green pepper and onion in hot oil till tender; stir in cornstarch. Add stewed tomatoes and tomato juice. Cook and stir till mixture is bubbly.

Add okra; return mixture to boiling. Reduce heat; cover and simmer for 10 minutes.

Add shrimp, crab-flavored fish, rice, and beef broth. Return mixture to boiling. Reduce heat. Cover and let stand about 5 minutes or till rice is tender, stirring occasionally. Makes 4 servings.

Nutrition information per serving: 259 calories, 20 g protein, 35 g carbohydrate, 5 g fat (1 g saturated), 116 mg cholesterol, 1,132 mg sodium, 787 mg potassium.

FISH AND VEGETABLE GAZPACHO

Chilled Gazpacho, often referred to as a Spanish "soup-salad," is perfect for hot summer nights. Serve it topped with some garlic croutons or with slices of toasted garlic bread.

12 ounces fresh *or* frozen skinless fish
     fillets (cod, grouper, *or* trout)
3   cups water
1   14½-ounce can vegetable *or* reduced-
     sodium chicken broth
½   teaspoon ground cumin
¼   teaspoon garlic powder
     Several dashes bottled hot pepper
     sauce
1   10-ounce can tomatoes with jalapeño
     peppers
1   small cucumber, chopped (1 cup)
1   small yellow summer squash *or*
     zucchini, chopped (1 cup)
2   plum tomatoes, chopped (1 cup)
2   to 3 green onions, sliced (¼ cup)

Thaw fish, if frozen. Rinse fish. Cut fish into ½-inch pieces.

In a medium saucepan bring water to boiling; add fish. Cover and simmer for 3 to 4 minutes or till fish flakes easily with a fork. Drain fish; cover and chill.

In a medium saucepan combine broth, cumin, garlic powder, and hot pepper sauce. Bring mixture to boiling. Remove from heat. Transfer to a large bowl. Stir in tomatoes with jalapeño peppers, cucumber, yellow summer squash or zucchini, plum tomatoes, and green onions. Cover and chill for 4 to 12 hours. Before serving, stir chilled fish into vegetable mixture. Makes 4 to 6 servings.

Nutrition information per serving: 124 calories, 16 g protein, 12 g carbohydrate, 2 g fat (0 g saturated), 33 mg cholesterol, 677 mg sodium, 506 mg potassium.

OYSTER-VEGETABLE CHOWDER

A chowder is a thick milk-based vegetable and seafood soup. The name comes from the French "chaudière," which refers to the large, heavy pots in which local fishermen cooked these soups.

½ of a 16-ounce package loose-pack frozen mixed broccoli, cauliflower, and carrots
1 medium onion, chopped (½ cup)
½ cup chicken *or* vegetable broth
⅛ teaspoon garlic salt
⅛ teaspoon white pepper
2 cups whole milk
1 cup half-and-half *or* light cream
1 pint shucked oysters *or* two 8-ounce cans whole oysters
2 to 3 teaspoons margarine *or* butter

Cut up any large frozen vegetables. In a 3-quart saucepan combine frozen vegetables, onion, chicken or vegetable broth, garlic salt, and white pepper. Bring mixture to boiling; reduce heat. Cover and simmer for 5 to 7 minutes or till vegetables are crisp-tender.

Stir milk and half-and-half or light cream into the vegetable mixture. Heat just to boiling. Add the *undrained* oysters. For fresh oysters, cook over medium heat about 5 minutes or till edges curl, stirring frequently. For canned oysters, cook till heated through.

Spoon into soup bowls. Top each serving with a little margarine or butter. Makes 4 to 6 servings.

Nutrition information per serving: 278 calories, 15 g protein, 19 g carbohydrate, 16 g fat (8 g saturated), 101 mg cholesterol, 417 mg sodium, 694 mg potassium.

QUICK ORIENTAL FISH SOUP

Skimp on time, not taste, when you serve this intriguing Asian-inspired soup.

12   ounces fresh *or* frozen monkfish, cusk,
     cod, *or* croaker fillets
 1   10¾-ounce can condensed chicken
     with rice soup
1½   cups water
 2   tablespoons reduced-sodium soy sauce
 ⅛   teaspoon ground red pepper
1½   cups loose-pack frozen broccoli, red
     pepper, onions, and mushrooms
 1   tablespoon lemon juice

Thaw fish, if frozen. Rinse fish. Cut into ½-inch pieces. Set fish aside.

In a large saucepan combine soup, water, soy sauce, and ground red pepper. Bring mixture to boiling. Add frozen vegetables. Return mixture to boiling; reduce heat. Cover and simmer for 5 minutes.

Add fish to saucepan. Cover and cook for 3 to 5 minutes more or till fish flakes easily with a fork. Stir in lemon juice. Makes 3 servings.

Nutrition information per serving: 155 calories, 23 g protein, 10 g carbohydrate, 2 g fat (1 g saturated), 48 mg cholesterol, 1,152 mg sodium, 410 mg potassium.

GRILLED SHRIMP AND PAPAYA SALAD

Choose an unblemished papaya that yields slightly to pressure. The skin of a ripe papaya may range in color from green to yellow to orange, but the flesh will be a brilliant coral color.

16   fresh *or* frozen jumbo shrimp in shells
       (about 1½ pounds)
½   cup plain yogurt
¼   cup mayonnaise *or* salad dressing
1   tablespoon honey
¾   teaspoon curry powder
⅛   teaspoon salt
     Leaf lettuce
1   cup shredded cucumber *or* zucchini
2   medium carrots, shredded (1 cup)
2   papayas (1½ pounds total), peeled,
       seeded, and thinly sliced
8   red *or* green sweet pepper rings
¼   cup sliced almonds, toasted (optional)

Thaw shrimp, if frozen. Set aside.

For dressing, in a small bowl stir together yogurt, mayonnaise or salad dressing, honey, curry powder, and salt. Chill till serving.

Remove shells from shrimp, leaving the tails intact. Devein shrimp. Rinse shrimp under cold running water. Pat dry with paper towels.

Thread shrimp onto metal skewers, leaving a ¼-inch space between pieces. Grill directly over medium coals for 10 to 12 minutes or till shrimp turn pink, turning skewers once. Brush shrimp lightly with some of the dressing. Remove shrimp from skewers.

Arrange lettuce leaves on 4 plates. Sprinkle *one-fourth* of the cucumber and *one-fourth* of the carrot over plate. Arrange shrimp, papaya, and pepper rings on each plate. Sprinkle with almonds. Serve with dressing. Makes 4 servings.

Nutrition information per serving: 390 calories, 25 g protein, 44 g carbohydrate, 13 g fat (2 g saturated), 203 mg cholesterol, 418 mg sodium, 1,066 mg potassium

SEAFOOD LOUIS SALAD

Using a blend of low-fat cottage cheese and skim milk, instead of the traditional mayonnaise and whipping cream, eliminates about 30 grams of fat and makes this classic salad completely guilt-free for fat-watchers.

1 6-ounce package frozen, peeled, cooked shrimp
½ cup low-fat cottage cheese
2 tablespoons skim milk
1 tablespoon tomato paste
2 tablespoons chopped red sweet pepper *or* diced pimiento
1 green onion, thinly sliced (2 tablespoons)
⅛ teaspoon salt
⅛ teaspoon pepper
Skim milk
6 cups torn romaine
1 cup shredded red cabbage (3 ounces)
1 medium carrot, shredded (½ cup)
1 6-ounce can crabmeat, drained, flaked, and cartilage removed (about 1½ cups)
2 tomatoes, cut into thin wedges
Carrot curls (optional)

Thaw shrimp, if frozen; set aside.

For dressing, in a blender container or food processor bowl combine low-fat cottage cheese, the 2 tablespoons milk, and tomato paste. Cover. Blend or process till smooth. Transfer to a small bowl. Stir in red pepper or pimiento, green onion, salt, pepper, and enough skim milk to make desired consistency. Cover and chill till serving time.

In a large bowl toss together romaine, red cabbage, and carrot. Divide among three salad plates. Arrange shrimp, crabmeat, and tomatoes on each plate. Drizzle with dressing. Garnish with carrot curls, if desired. Pass any remaining dressing. Makes 3 servings.

Nutrition information per serving: 207 calories, 31 g protein, 14 g carbohydrate, 3 g fat (1 g saturated), 171 mg cholesterol, 729 mg sodium, 921 mg potassium

ORIENTAL SPINACH TUNA SALAD

Japanese rice vinegar has a pale straw color and mild flavor. In a pinch, substitute white wine vinegar.

6 cups torn spinach
1 9¼-ounce can water-pack tuna, chilled, drained, and broken into large pieces
1 cup fresh bean sprouts
1 8-ounce can sliced water chestnuts, drained
1 large tomato, cut into wedges
1 stalk celery, chopped (½ cup)
1 green onion, sliced (2 tablespoons)
3 tablespoons soy sauce
2 tablespoons rice vinegar *or* white wine vinegar
1 tablespoon water
2 to 3 teaspoons toasted sesame oil
1 teaspoon sugar
⅛ teaspoon dry mustard
   Several dashes bottled hot pepper sauce

In a large salad bowl combine spinach, tuna, bean sprouts, water chestnuts, tomato wedges, celery, and green onion. Toss to mix.

For dressing, in a screw-top jar combine soy sauce, rice vinegar or white wine vinegar, water, sesame oil, sugar, dry mustard, and bottled hot pepper sauce. Cover and shake to mix well.

Pour dressing over spinach mixture. Toss to coat. Makes 4 servings.

Nutrition information per serving: 172 calories, 24 g protein, 14 g carbohydrate, 3 g fat (1 g saturated), 12 mg cholesterol, 1,095 mg sodium, 928 mg potassium

GREEK SHRIMP SALAD

Anchovies are small saltwater fish noted for their intense flavor. Most are cured in salt, then canned in oil or brine, which gives them a salty flavor.

1   8-ounce package frozen, peeled,
      cooked shrimp
4   cups torn romaine
2   cups torn iceberg *or* leaf lettuce
2   small tomatoes, chopped (1 cup)
¾   cup crumbled feta cheese (3 ounces)
2   green onions, sliced (¼ cup)
¼   cup sliced pitted ripe olives
⅓   cup olive oil *or* salad oil
⅓   cup white wine vinegar
2   teaspoons snipped fresh oregano *or*
      ½ teaspoon dried oregano, crushed
⅛   teaspoon garlic powder
⅛   teaspoon pepper
1   2-ounce can anchovy fillets, drained
      (optional)

Thaw shrimp, if frozen. Set aside.

In a large bowl toss together romaine and iceberg or leaf lettuce. Arrange greens on four individual salad plates. Top with shrimp, tomatoes, feta cheese, green onions, and olives.

For dressing, in a screw-top jar, combine olive oil or salad oil, vinegar, oregano, garlic powder, and pepper. Cover and shake well to mix. Pour dressing over salads. Top with the anchovy fillets, if desired. Makes 4 servings.

Nutrition information per serving: 310 calories, 17 g protein, 7 g carbohydrate, 25 g fat (6 g saturated), 130 mg cholesterol, 423 mg sodium, 490 mg potassium

TROPICAL SCALLOP SALAD

Sea scallops are larger than either bay or calico scallops. Cut any of the large scallops so they will cook evenly.

1   pound fresh *or* frozen sea scallops
1   15¼-ounce can pineapple spears
2   tablespoons white wine vinegar
1½ teaspoons sugar
¼   teaspoon shredded lime peel
1½ teaspoons lime juice
1   teaspoon cornstarch
⅛   teaspoon ground cinnamon
⅛   teaspoon ground cumin
1   cup sugar snap peas
1   medium head Boston *or* Bibb lettuce
    (6 to 7 ounces)
1   medium mango, peeled, seeded, and
    sliced
½   medium carrot, finely shredded
    (¼ cup)

Thaw scallops, if frozen. Set aside.

For dressing, drain pineapple, reserving ⅓ cup of the juice. In a small saucepan combine the reserved pineapple juice, white wine vinegar, sugar, lime peel, lime juice, cornstarch, cinnamon, and cumin. Cook and stir till mixture is thickened and bubbly. Cook and stir for 2 minutes more. Remove from heat; cool.

Cook sugar snap peas in a small amount of boiling water for 1 minute. Drain and cool.

Rinse scallops. Cut any large scallops in half. Cook scallops in lightly salted boiling water for 1 to 3 minutes or till opaque. Drain.

Line four individual salad plates with lettuce leaves. Arrange scallops on one side of each plate. From scallops, fan out pineapple spears, mango slices, and sugar snap peas. Drizzle with dressing. Sprinkle with shredded carrot. Makes 4 servings.

Nutrition information per serving: 221 calories, 17 g protein, 39 g carbohydrate, 1 g fat (0 g saturated), 34 mg cholesterol, 178 mg sodium, 771 mg potassium

EASY PAELLA SALAD

Turmeric, although unrelated to saffron, provides a similar intense golden color for a fraction of the cost, in this easy, make-ahead salad.

1   6-ounce package frozen, peeled, cooked shrimp
½   cup frozen peas
1   6½-ounce jar marinated artichoke hearts
2   cups cold cooked rice
1   6½ ounce can chopped clams, drained
¼   cup Italian salad dressing
⅛   teaspoon ground turmeric
12 whole cherry tomatoes, halved (about 1 cup)
    Lettuce leaves (optional)

Thaw shrimp and peas; set aside.

Drain artichoke hearts, reserving marinade. In a large bowl combine shrimp, peas, artichoke hearts, rice, and clams. Toss to mix.

For dressing, in a screw top jar combine reserved artichoke marinade, Italian dressing, and turmeric. Cover and shake well. Pour over shrimp mixture. Toss gently to coat.

Cover and chill till serving (up to 4 hours). Just before serving, gently stir cherry tomatoes into shrimp mixture. Line salad plates with lettuce leaves. Serve shrimp mixture on lettuce-lined plates. Makes 4 servings.

Nutrition information per serving: 375 calories, 18 g protein, 46 g carbohydrate, 14 g fat (1 g saturated), 122 mg cholesterol, 502 mg sodium, 403 mg potassium

MARINATED SQUID SALAD WITH DRIED TOMATOES

Members of the onion family, shallots look like large, brown garlic bulbs. More expensive than the average onion, their unique and delicate flavor is well worth the extra cost.

1   pound cleaned squid
¼   cup olive oil *or* cooking oil
1   tablespoon chopped shallots
1   clove garlic, minced
½   teaspoon finely shredded orange peel
¼   cup orange juice
2   tablespoons tarragon vinegar
4   oil-packed dried tomatoes, cut into thin strips
3   cups torn romaine (about 5 ounces)
3   cups torn leaf lettuce (about 5 ounces)
1   small cucumber, halved lengthwise and thinly sliced (1½ cups)
1   small red sweet pepper, cut into thin strips (½ cup)

Rinse squid. Pat dry with paper towels. Cut squid into thin rings.

In a large skillet heat *2 tablespoons* of the oil. Cook squid, shallots, and garlic in hot oil for 2 to 3 minutes or till squid is opaque. Drain excess liquid.

Transfer squid and vegetables to a medium mixing bowl. Stir in remaining oil, orange peel, orange juice, vinegar, and tomato strips. Toss to mix. Cover and chill for 1 to 2 hours.

To serve, in a large salad bowl toss together romaine, leaf lettuce, cucumber, and red sweet pepper. Add squid mixture. Toss to mix. Makes 4 servings.

Nutrition information per serving: 277 calories, 20 g protein, 14 g carbohydrate, 16 g fat (3 g saturated), 264 mg cholesterol, 78 mg sodium, 817 mg potassium

WARM SPINACH AND SCALLOP SALAD

As summer turns to fall, cut the cool edge on the weather with a warm blend of mixed greens, tender scallops, and crunchy nuts.

12 ounces fresh *or* frozen bay scallops
 4 cups torn fresh spinach (5 ounces)
 4 cups torn Boston *or* Bibb lettuce
     (about 6 ounces)
 1 small red sweet pepper, cut into thin
     strips (½ cup)
 ½ medium carrot, shredded (¼ cup)
 3 tablespoons water
 2 tablespoons lemon juice
 2 tablespoons honey
 1 tablespoon prepared mustard
 2 tablespoons cooking oil
 2 tablespoons minced shallots
 ¼ cup chopped pecans, toasted

Thaw scallops, if frozen; set aside.

In a large salad bowl combine spinach, Boston or Bibb lettuce, red sweet pepper, and carrot. Set aside.

For dressing, in a screw-top jar combine water, lemon juice, honey, and mustard. Cover and shake well. Set aside.

In a large skillet heat oil over medium-high heat. Add scallops and shallots. Cook and stir for 1 to 3 minutes or till scallops are opaque. Remove scallops with slotted spoon. Add scallops to salad bowl.

Shake dressing again. Pour dressing into skillet. Heat just to boiling. Pour dressing mixture over mixture in salad bowl; toss gently to mix. Sprinkle with toasted chopped pecans. Serve immediately. Makes 4 servings.

Nutrition information per serving: 198 calories, 14 g protein, 17 g carbohydrate, 9 g fat (1 g saturated), 25 mg cholesterol, 228 mg sodium, 781 mg potassium

CRAB AND PEAR SALAD

For an extra splash of color, use the meat from freshly-cooked crab claws instead of the canned crab.

2 6½-ounce cans crabmeat, drained, flaked, and cartilage removed (1½ cups)
½ cup seedless red grapes, halved
1 stalk celery, chopped (½ cup)
½ cup cubed Swiss cheese (2 ounces)
⅓ cup dairy sour cream *or* plain yogurt
⅓ cup mayonnaise *or* salad dressing
½ teaspoon finely shredded lemon peel
1 teaspoon lemon juice
 Leaf lettuce *and/or* purple flowering kale
1 large pear, cored and sliced
¼ cup pecans, toasted

In a medium bowl combine crabmeat, grapes, celery, and Swiss cheese cubes. Set aside.

For dressing, in a small bowl stir together sour cream or yogurt, mayonnaise or salad dressing, lemon peel, and lemon juice. Mix well.

Pour dressing over crab mixture. Toss gently to coat.

Line four salad plates with leaf lettuce and/or purple flowering kale. Arrange pear slices on plates. Spoon crab mixture onto greens. Sprinkle with pecans. Makes 4 servings.

Nutrition information per serving: 366 calories, 15 g protein, 14 g carbohydrate, 29 g fat (8 g saturated), 83 mg cholesterol, 422 mg sodium, 308 mg potassium

FRUITED TUNA SALAD

If the strawberries are especially large, try slicing them instead of halving them.

1   8-ounce carton vanilla yogurt
1   teaspoon finely shredded orange peel
1   11-ounce can mandarin orange
     sections, drained, *or* 2 oranges,
     peeled and sectioned
1½   cups cubed cantaloupe *or* honeydew
     melon
1½   cups halved strawberries
2   7-ounce cans solid white tuna,
     drained and coarsely flaked
     Leaf lettuce
¼   cup chopped pecans, toasted

In a large bowl stir together vanilla yogurt and orange peel. Add orange sections, cantaloupe or honeydew melon, and strawberries. Toss gently to coat. Add tuna. Toss lightly again.

To serve, line four salad plates with lettuce. Arrange tuna mixture on the lettuce-lined plates. Sprinkle with pecans. Makes 4 servings.

Nutrition information per serving: 296 calories, 27 g protein, 31 g carbohydrate, 8 g fat (2 g saturated), 38 mg cholesterol, 382 mg sodium, 774 mg potassium

TUNA SPINACH BRAID

Impressive, yet easy to make—an entertainer's delight. The filling can be made ahead of time and chilled to save last minute preparation.

1   10-ounce package frozen chopped
      spinach, thawed and well drained
1   9¼-ounce can chunk white tuna
      (water pack), drained and flaked
1   cup ricotta cheese *or* cream-style
      cottage cheese, drained
½   cup grated Parmesan cheese
1   clove garlic, minced
1   package (8) refrigerated crescent rolls
3   thick slices provolone cheese
      (3 ounces)
    Chopped tomato (optional)
    Grated Parmesan cheese (optional)

For filling, in a large bowl combine spinach, tuna, ricotta or cottage cheese, ½ cup Parmesan cheese, and garlic; set aside.

Unroll and separate the crescent dough into 4 rectangles. On an ungreased baking sheet or shallow baking pan, place rectangles together, overlapping edges slightly, to form a 14x10-inch rectangle. Firmly press edges and perforations together to seal.

Spread filling in a 3½-inch-wide strip, lengthwise down the center of dough. Top with provolone cheese, cutting cheese as necessary to cover the length of the filling.

Make cuts in dough at 1-inch intervals on both long sides of rectangle just to the edge of the filling. Fold dough strips diagonally over filling, overlapping strips and alternating from side to side to give a braided appearance.

Bake in a 375° oven for 18 to 20 minutes or till golden. Serve warm. If deisred, serve with chopped tomatoes and additional grated Parmesan cheese. Makes 4 main-dish or 8 appetizer servings.

Nutrition information per serving: 518 calories, 40 g protein, 29 g carbohydrate, 28 g fat (11 g saturated), 70 mg cholesterol, 1,245 mg sodium, 575 mg potassium

SUBMARINE TUNA SANDWICH

The hoagie buns may be slightly shorter than French rolls, but either works well in this hefty sandwich.

1 cup finely shredded cabbage
⅓ cup mayonnaise *or* salad dressing
½ teaspoon finely shredded lemon *or* lime peel
1 tablespoon lemon *or* lime juice
1 tablespoon snipped chives
1 6½-ounce can tuna (water pack), drained and broken into chunks
4 French rolls *or* hoagie buns (each 7 inches long)
2 tomatoes, thinly sliced
1 small cucumber, thinly sliced
4 slices Swiss cheese, halved (4 ounces)

For tuna filling, in a mixing bowl combine cabbage, mayonnaise or salad dressing, lemon or lime peel, lemon or lime juice, and snipped chives. Gently stir in tuna. Set aside.

Split French rolls or hoagie buns horizontally. Line bottoms of rolls with tomato slices. Divide tuna filling evenly among the rolls. Top with the thinly sliced cucumber. Add Swiss cheese slices and roll tops. Cut sandwiches crosswise in half. Serve with additional tomato slices and cucumber slices, if desired. Makes 4 servings.

Nutrition information per serving: 712 calories, 33 g protein, 82 g carbohydrate, 28 g fat (8 g saturated), 54 mg cholesterol, 1,116 mg sodium, 573 mg potassium

SALMON BURGERS WITH BASIL MAYONNAISE

Fresh basil is the secret ingredient in both this burger and its refreshing mayonnaise topping.

1	beaten egg
¾	cup soft whole wheat bread crumbs (1 slice)
4	teaspoons snipped fresh basil
¼	teaspoon pepper
1	6½-ounce can skinless, boneless salmon, drained and flaked
½	medium carrot, finely shredded (¼ cup)
¼	cup finely shredded Gruyère *or* Swiss cheese (1 ounce)
2	tablespoons mayonnaise *or* salad dressing
1	tablespoon dairy sour cream
2	teaspoons snipped fresh basil
1	teaspoon finely shredded lemon peel
3	lettuce leaves
3	slices rye *or* whole wheat bread, toasted
	Tomato wedges (optional)

In a large mixing bowl combine egg, bread crumbs, 4 teaspoons basil, and pepper. Add salmon, carrot, and cheese. Mix lightly. Shape salmon mixture into three ¾-inch-thick round patties.

Place salmon patties on a lightly greased baking sheet. Broil patties about 3 inches from the heat about 8 minutes or till heated through and light brown, carefully turning patties once after 4 minutes.

Meanwhile, for the basil mayonnaise, combine mayonnaise or salad dressing, sour cream, 2 teaspoons basil, and lemon peel.

Place a lettuce leaf on each slice of toasted bread. Top each with a salmon burger and some of the basil mayonnaise. Serve with tomato wedges, if desired. Makes 3 servings.

Nutrition information per serving: 297 calories, 20 g protein, 24 g carbohydrate, 13 g fat (4 g saturated), 115 mg cholesterol, 658 mg sodium, 595 mg potassium

CLAM AND BACON BUNDLES

Brushing the tops of the bundles with milk before baking makes them even more crispy and irresistibly golden brown.

2   slices bacon
¾   cup finely chopped broccoli
         (4 to 5 ounces)
1   medium shredded carrot (½ cup)
1   small yellow summer squash, chopped
         (1 cup)
2   6½-ounce cans chopped clams,
         drained
⅓   cup soft-style cream cheese with
         chives and onion
2   tablespoons creamy cucumber salad
         dressing
1   10-ounce package refrigerated pizza
         dough
1   tablespoon milk
1   tablespoon sesame seed

In a large skillet cook bacon till crisp. Remove bacon, reserving 1 tablespoon drippings in skillet. Drain bacon on paper towels. Crumble; set aside.

For filling, cook broccoli and carrot in reserved drippings for 2 minutes. Add squash; cook for 1 minute more. Remove from heat. Stir in clams, cream cheese, salad dressing, and crumbled bacon. Set aside.

On a lightly floured surface, roll pizza dough to a 12x12-inch square. Cut dough into four 6-inch squares. Place ½ *cup* of the filling on one corner of *each* square. Moisten edges and fold opposite corner over filling. Press edges with tines of fork to seal. Brush bundles with milk. Sprinkle with sesame seed.

Place bundles on a greased baking sheet. Bake in a 400° oven about 20 minutes or till golden. Cool on a wire rack for 5 minutes. Serve warm. Makes 4 servings.

Nutrition information per serving: 390 calories, 23 g protein, 35 g carbohydrate, 18 g fat (5 g saturated), 57 mg cholesterol, 494 mg sodium, 671 mg potassium

COOL AND CREAMY COD SANDWICHES

It's the horseradish mustard, a condiment often used to enhance the flavor of seafood, that puts the zip into this anything but ordinary sandwich.

12 ounces fresh *or* frozen cod fillets
½ stalk celery, finely chopped (¼ cup)
¼ cup mayonnaise *or* salad dressing
1 green onion, sliced (2 tablespoons)
1 to 2 tablespoons horseradish mustard
1 tablespoon lemon juice
¼ teaspoon pepper
   Dash ground red pepper (optional)
4 individual French rolls
1 cup shredded lettuce (about 2 ounces)

Thaw fish, if frozen. Rinse fish.

Pour ¾-inch of water into a large saucepan or Dutch oven. Place a steamer basket over the water. Bring to boiling. Gently lay fish in basket, cutting to fit, if necessary. Cover and steam fish for 6 to 8 minutes or till fish flakes easily with a fork.

Remove fish from steamer basket. Pat fish dry with paper towels. Place fish in a large bowl. Using a fork, flake fish into small pieces. Stir in celery, mayonnaise or salad dressing, green onion, horseradish mustard, lemon juice, and pepper. Mix till combined. Cover and chill for 1 hour.

To assemble sandwiches, split French rolls horizontally. Place *one-fourth* of the shredded lettuce inside each bun. Top each with *one-fourth* of the chilled cod mixture. Makes 4 servings.

Nutrition information per serving: 317 calories, 23 g protein, 25 g carbohydrate, 14 g fat (2 g saturated), 50 mg cholesterol, 418 mg sodium, 303 mg potassium

Keep track of your daily nutrition needs by using the information we provide at the end of each recipe. We've analyzed the nutritional content of each recipe serving for you. When a recipe gives an ingredient substitution, we used the first choice in the analysis. If it makes a range of servings (such as 4 to 6), we used the smallest number. Ingredients listed as optional weren't included in the calculations.

METRIC COOKING HINTS

By making a few conversions, cooks in Australia, Canada, and the United Kingdom can use the recipes in Better Homes and Gardens® *Pizzas* with confidence. The charts on this page provide a guide for converting measurements from the U.S. customary system, which is used throughout this book, to the imperial and metric systems. There also is a conversion table for oven temperatures to accommodate the differences in oven calibrations.

Volume and Weight: Americans traditionally use cup measures for liquid and solid ingredients. The chart (top right) shows the approximate imperial and metric equivalents. If you are accustomed to weighing solid ingredients, here are some helpful approximate equivalents.

■ 1 cup butter, caster sugar, or rice = 8 ounces = about 250 grams
■ 1 cup flour = 4 ounces = about 125 grams
■ 1 cup icing sugar = 5 ounces = about 150 grams

Spoon measures are used for smaller amounts of ingredients although the size of the tablespoon varies slightly among countries, for practical purposes and for recipes in this book, a straight substitution is all that's necessary.

Measurements made using cups or spoons should always be level, unless stated otherwise.

Product Differences: Most of the ingredients called for in the recipes in this book are available in English-speaking countries. However, some are known by different names. Here are some common American ingredients and their possible counterparts:

■ Sugar is granulated or caster sugar.
■ Powdered sugar is icing sugar.
■ All-purpose flour is plain household flour or white flour. When self-rising flour is used in place of all-purpose flour in a recipe that calls for leavening, omit the leavening agent (baking soda or baking powder) and salt.
■ Light corn syrup is golden syrup.
■ Cornstarch is cornflour.
■ Baking soda is bicarbonate of soda.
■ Vanilla is vanilla essence.

USEFUL EQUIVALENTS

⅛ teaspoon = 0.5 ml
¼ teaspoon = 1 ml
½ teaspoon = 2 ml
1 teaspoon = 5 ml
¼ cup = 2 fluid ounces = 50 ml
⅓ cup = 3 fluid ounces = 75 ml
½ cup = 4 fluid ounces = 125 ml

⅔ cup = 5 fluid ounces = 150 ml
¾ cup = 6 fluid ounces = 175 ml
1 cup = 8 fluid ounces = 250 ml
2 cups = 1 pint
2 pints = 1 litre
½ inch = 1 centimetre
1 inch = 2 centimetres

BAKING PAN SIZES

American	Metric
8x1½-inch round baking pan	20x4-centimetre sandwich or cake tin
9x1½-inch round baking pan	23x3.5-centimetre sandwich or cake tin
11x7x1½-inch baking pan	28x18x4-centimetre baking pan
13x9x2-inch baking pan	32.5x23x5-centimetre baking pan
2-quart rectangular baking dish	30x19x5-centimetre baking pan
15x10x2-inch baking pan	38x25.5x2.5-centimetre baking pan (Swiss roll tin)
9-inch pie plate	22x4- or 23x4-centimetre pie plate
7- or 8-inch springform pan	18- or 20-centimetre springform or loose-bottom cake tin
9x5x3-inch loaf pan	23x13x6-centimetre or 2-pound narrow loaf pan or paté tin
1½-quart casserole	1.5-litre casserole
2-quart casserole	2-litre casserole

OVEN TEMPERATURE EQUIVALENTS

Fahrenheit Setting	Celsius Setting*	Gas Setting
300°F	150°C	Gas Mark 2
325°F	160°C	Gas Mark 3
350°F	180°C	Gas Mark 4
375°F	190°C	Gas Mark 5
400°F	200°C	Gas Mark 6
425°F	220°C	Gas Mark 7
450°F	230°C	Gas Mark 8
Broil		Grill

Electric and gas ovens may be calibrated using Celsius. However, increase the Celsius setting 10 to 20 degrees when cooking above 160°C with an electric oven. For convection or forced-air ovens (gas or electric), lower the temperature setting 10°C when cooking at all heat levels.